It's not that America is not in the Bible—
it's that we don't know who we are."—
so says author and teacher, Daniel Bilbro.
In this first book of the ***American
Prophecy Series***, the author lays the
foundation and illumination of Scripture
upon that most noble of nations that has
ever existed in the history of mankind—
the United States of America.

Join us at our website,
Patriot Passion—Patriot Hope, at:
www.patriotpassion.com

CONFLICT OF THE AGES

by Daniel Bilbro

Published by
Patriot Passion—Patriot Hope
www.patriotpassion.com.

Copyright © 2007 by Daniel Bilbro

Notice of Rights All rights reserved. No part of this book may be reproduced or transmitted in any form by any means, electronic, mechanical, photocopying, recording, or otherwise, without the prior written permission of the publisher. For information on getting permission for reprints and excerpts, go to www.patriotpassion.com

ISBN 978-0-615-36847-4

Printed and bound in the United States of America

DEDICATION AND THANKS

Thanks to A.S. Bell for your editing (multiple times).

Many thanks to Don and Judy T., my pastors for life.

To my friends Allen & Margo for reading and encouraging me through all of these writings and for a friendship that has lasted several decades.

To my new friend Dwayne, a true example of the humility of Christ. Your constant encouragement and faith has made all the difference my friend.

Last but certainly not least, to my beloved friend and wife of 34 years, Sherry. You have taught me the true meaning of grace, faith, and forgiveness. Without you it is doubtful that I would have written this book.

INTRODUCTION

When one attempts to overturn 1,700 years of a prevailing Biblical teaching that has been widely accepted by notable and honorable Christian leaders—both Protestant and Catholic—a proper respect for the opinions of these leaders requires me to declare the reasons that compel me to refute this teaching and to present an alternate and more precise interpretation. I submit to the reader that the true interpretation of chapters 11 and 12 of the prophet Daniel are more incredible than has heretofore been imagined. As a young Christian, I read the traditional interpretations of Daniel, and even at my young and ignorant age some things just didn't seem to fit. "If the prophets were so gifted," I asked, "why did they miss all the really big and important events in history?" Now, after almost four decades and thousands of hours of prayer and study later, I offer for the reader's consideration the astonishing truth of chapters 11 and 12 of the book of Daniel.

This teaching will, like a roller-coaster ride, seem a bit slow in that initial climb to the top—but continue to the end of the ride, and I promise it will be worth the effort. This book is broken into two distinct sections. The first section, *Deconstructing the Traditional Interpretation*, summarizes the traditional interpretation of these two chapters of Daniel, and then, against this long-held belief, I present arguments both historical and theological. The second section, *The Conflict Begins*, is a presentation of what I contend to be the true interpretation of chapters 11 and 12 of the book of Daniel.

My earnest prayer is that this book, along with others that are soon to follow, will strengthen the hearts of true believers worldwide with the reality of the undeniable Divine authorship of the Bible and demonstrate the absolute intellectual dishonesty of the skeptic. For in Daniel chapter 11 from verses 2 through 38 are a remarkable 108 chronologically accurate predictions of the unfolding of major, civilization-shattering events spanning almost 2,600 years of human history. These events began in the time of Daniel's writings under the reign of Cyrus the Great of Persia, circa 600 B.C., and continue even unto this present hour. The interpretation presented here of Daniel's writings is not mere opinion but a logical correlation and merging of two realities—the reality of the irrefutable Biblical, prophetic truth linked with the reality of incontrovertible, historical facts.

Regarding the gift of revelation contained in these pages, I am humbled by God's favor, and am continually in awe of His wondrous grace. For He still chooses the weak and foolish things to confound the wise and learned. Nevertheless, I echo the Apostle Paul in stating, *"I neither received it from man nor was I taught it, but I was taught it by a revelation of Jesus Christ"* (Galatians 1:12). I do not make this claim to add weight or authority to the teaching contained herein; it is for you the reader to logically decide these things for yourself. I make this statement, however, to give glory and honor to my Lord and Savior, Jesus Christ who has revealed these mysteries to one such as myself.

I identify with Patrick of Ireland, who in A.D. 450 wrote:

...I was like a stone lying in deep mire, and He that is mighty came and in His mercy raised me up and, indeed, lifted me high up and placed me on top of the wall. And from there I ought to shout out in gratitude to the Lord for His great favors in this world and forever, that the mind of man cannot measure. Therefore be amazed, you great and small who fear God...Who was it summoned me, a fool, from the midst of those who appear wise and learned...? Me, truly wretched in this world...with fear and reverence, and faithfully, without complaint, would come to the people to whom the love of Christ brought me and gave me in my lifetime, if I should be worthy, to serve them truly and with humility.[1]

I remain forever in Christ's service,

Daniel Bilbro

"For the earth shall be filled with the knowledge of the glory of the Lord, as the waters cover the sea." Habakkuk 2:14

ACKNOWLEDGEMENTS & EXPLANATIONS

All Biblical quotations are from the New American Standard Bible unless noted otherwise. The following abbreviations thus apply: HNV = Hebrew Names Version; NWV = Noah Webster Version; JDT = J. Darby Translation; RYT = Robert Young Literal Translation; KJV = King James Version.

My acknowledgement and thanks to www.eliyah.com/lexicon.html along with www.blueletterbible.org for maintaining excellent Biblical resource sites including Strong's Concordance and Thayer's Lexicon.

Daniel states in 12:4 *"...conceal these words until the end of time...knowledge will increase..."* I believe that it is highly probable that these two statements are interrelated. For in spite of all of the evil that is vomited out of the internet, without the readily available historical resource and "increase of knowledge" that is available through this media it is doubtful that this book could have been written. For this reason, except in cases where specific websites were difficult to find, I have chosen not to include many historical end-note references since these will be easily verifiable through Google or other search engines.

NOTE– For the sake of brevity throughout the book, I have standardized the following formatting conventions:
- All Biblical quotes will be italicized.
- Hebrew word 'pronunciations' and 'definitions' will also be italicized
- My comments along with the correlating historical events will be in standard text
- {Relevant historical events that fill the gaps in the historical chronology but do not directly correspond to Daniel's prophecy will be in brackets.} These are given in order to add needed context to the flow of historical events.

---

[1] The Declaration of Saint Patrick

THE TRADITIONAL INTERPRETATION
THE HELLENISTIC WORLD IN 275 BC

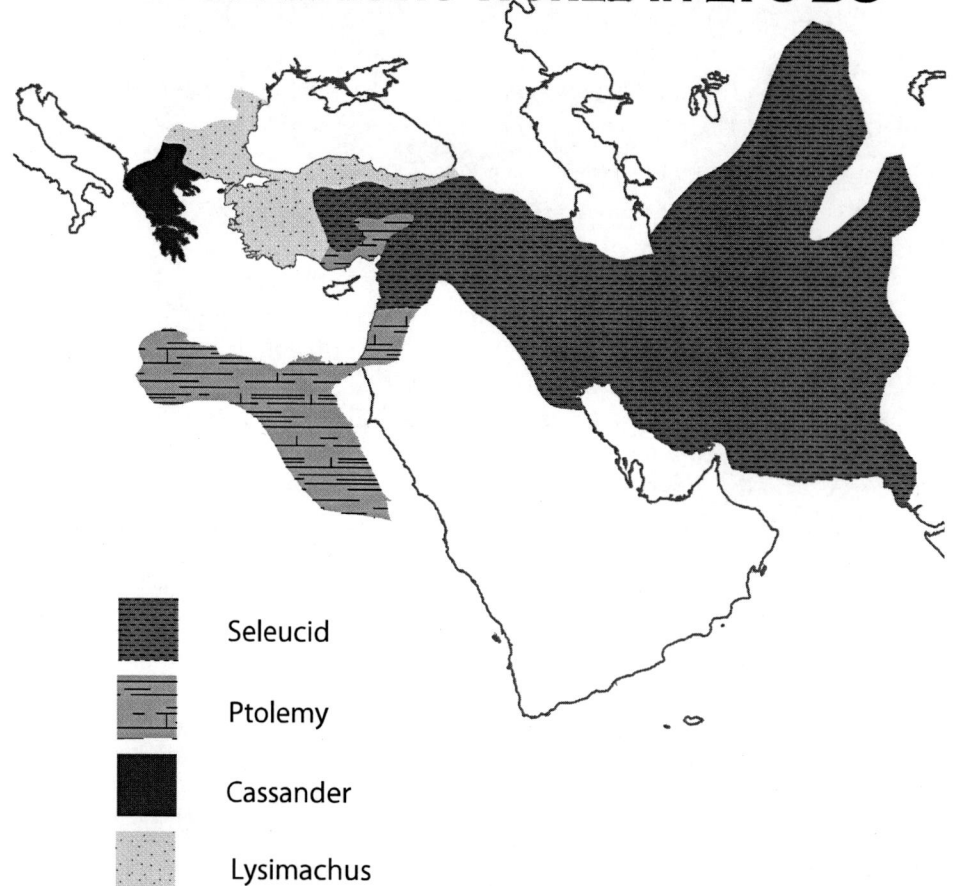

- Seleucid
- Ptolemy
- Cassander
- Lysimachus

DECONSTRUCTING THE TRADITIONAL INTERPRETATION:

Part 1—What's wrong with this picture?

In chapter 11 of his book, Daniel relates the Divine visions given to him along with the interpretations as explained to him by the angel Gabriel. In verses 1-4, Gabriel explains to Daniel about the outcome of the Persian Empire (the prevailing world power at the time) and of the coming of the unstoppable armies of Greece, which with the benefit of historical sight we know were led by Alexander the Great. Then beginning in verse 5, the prophet Daniel speaks in detail regarding conflicts between *"the king of the North"* and *"the king of the South,"* and this is where I am forced to disagree with the traditional view that has managed to survive for almost 1700 years.

The traditional interpretation of verses 5 through 35 is universally accepted to relate in great detail the forthcoming conflicts between two of the generals of Alexander the Great who succeeded him and carved up his conquests. Alexander himself died at the early age of 32 in Babylon, the victim either of disease or of poisoning or of pneumonia brought about by aspiration of his own vomit after a drunken orgy (depending upon which historical account one chooses to believe). Alexander's only legitimate heir was soon murdered, and four of Alexander's generals/boyhood friends partitioned the kingdom but not without conflict. Per the traditional Interpretation, the *"king of the South"* is accepted to be the Ptolemy dynasty of Egypt founded by Ptolemy Soter, and the *"king of the North"* is accepted to be the Seleucid dynasty of Babylon and Persia (and later Syria) as established by Seleucus Nicator.[2]

What is truly surprising is that this universally accepted, traditional interpretation was not originally authored by a Christian at all but rather was first submitted in writing by the pagan Syrian philosopher Porphyrius in his work *Adversus Christianos*[3] (Against Christians). Writing in the late 200's A.D., Porphyrius asserts that portions of the book of Daniel reflected historical events too accurately and therefore could not have been written by Daniel as claimed (ca. 530 BC), but were written by Jewish scribes translating the Septuagint (Hebrew-to-Greek Old Testament) during the time of Antiochus Epiphanies (ca. 215 BC) in the twilight years of the Greek empire. Thus Porphyrius alleged that the prophetic portions of the book of Daniel were not prophetic at all, but were instead historic and therefore fraudulent. He did this in order to slander and discredit the early Christians, their writings, and their God. How ironic that this pagan interpretation should come to be accepted by Christians as the correct and authentic view of prophetic fulfillment.

Porphyrius's conclusions were soundly refuted by his contemporary Eusebius, the bishop of Caesarea, and later by St. Jerome in 342 A.D. (translator of the *Latin Vulgate* version of the Bible) who correctly defended the authenticity and authorship of Daniel. However, Jerome was swayed by the Syrian's historical correlations and proceeded to write a detailed commentary on this chapter based on the interpretation of Porphyrius. With only minor disagreements, Jerome's interpretation has been stud-

---

[2] For reference, the two other generals that do not come into this prophecy were Cassander, who ruled over the Greek homeland; and Lysimachus, who ruled over Asia Minor for a relatively brief time period.
[3] http://www.attalus.org/translate/daniel.html

ied and quoted by many Christian leaders through the ages including John Calvin (c.1540), Matthew Henry (1714), and Jameison, Fauset & Brown (1871). It is advanced to this present day by Pastor Ray Stedman (deceased 1992) of *Peninsula Bible Church*, Palo Alto, CA; Pastor Chuck Smith of *Calvary Chapel*; Dr. John Walvoord of *Dallas Theological Seminary*; noted radio personality Pastor Chuck Swindol, and many others. This predominant interpretation is taught and accepted seemingly without question in most Bible schools, seminaries, and Christian churches throughout the western world.

Although I respect the character of many of the Christian leaders I have just mentioned, I must disagree on intellectual grounds with the conclusion they have formed in regards to this particular prophetical passage of scripture. So not to belabor the point, let me emphasize that my writing is an intellectual disagreement—not character disagreement.

So why has the traditional interpretation managed to survive for so many centuries? In part because it appears to fit well and thus, I assume, has never been seriously questioned or re-examined. I say it appears to fit well when in actuality it does not. It fits as well as my dinner-suit would fit on the body of a ten-year-old boy. Yes, the arms and legs all come out the right places and it is tailored to fit a *homo-sapien* not *canine-domesticus*. But here the history of the Ptolemies and the Seleucids clothed in the prophecy of Daniel becomes awkward and unkempt. For in order to make the prophecy fit the aforementioned age of history, it must be taken in here, decreased in girth there, and the sleeves and pants' legs rolled-up. In short, it must be tweaked and fiddled with by the "tailor" with the hope that the near-sighted consumer will not stand too close to the mirror.

It is necessary to totally eviscerate this traditional interpretation for two reasons. Firstly, it is wrong. It is wrong historically and it is wrong theologically. Secondly, and just as importantly, it reinforces a widespread mistaken belief that many prophecies have a "double fulfillment." That is, they were fulfilled (at least in part) at some point in the past and will be fulfilled again, or in their entirety, in the future. Usually these "future" events are thrown into the bucket of "The Great Tribulation Period" or the bucket of the "Millennial Reign of Christ" since we are apparently rapidly running out of history and time for these events to unfold. However, this "double fulfillment" quandary flies in direct contradiction to the New Testament admonition, *"But know this first of all, that no prophecy of Scripture is a matter of one's own interpretation, for no prophecy was ever made by an act of human will, but men moved by the Holy Spirit spoke from God"* (2 Peter 1:20, 21). In my studies of commentaries that reflect this belief, it seems to be less of a "double fulfillment" issue and more of an example of *eisigesis*—that is, reading something into the scriptural passage that one wants to find there.

I am not saying that there aren't lessons to be learned regarding life, sin, and the nature of God in an allegorical sense from a particular prophecy, but rather that there can be only one literal fulfillment for any particular prophetic passage. Equally important, and I cannot stress this enough, not only must prophecy be fulfilled, but also it is meant to be observed and witnessed as being fulfilled. This principle, which I call *"mandatory prophetic witness"*, eliminates the supposed completion of prophecies that occurred in some dusty corner of the world only to be observed by a few nomads wandering the deserts of the *Rub al Khali* of the Arabian Peninsula or the *An-Nafud* of Syria. God wants the fulfillment of the written word to be witnessed by all the world for a testimony—a testimony to the greatness of Yahweh and a testimony to the accuracy of prophecies that were written hundreds or thousands of years before they come to pass. For He says through Isaiah,

"...I am God, and there is none like me, declaring the end from the beginning, and from ancient times the things that are not yet done, saying, My counsel shall stand, and I will do all my pleasure:" Isaiah 46:9b, 10.

And again in the book of Jeremiah, God states through the prophet,

"...I am watching over My word to perform it." Jeremiah 1:12

Fulfilled prophecy bears witness to the greatness and uniqueness of our God. Who else but He can declare to us events that are coming to pass in this present day from the voices of prophets spoken over 2 millennia ago?

Part 2—Problems of a theological nature:

Firstly, there is a problem with the time-scale per verse that is inconsistent in the Traditional Interpretation. For example, Daniel encompasses the remaining 200 years of the Persian Empire in only half of one verse—verse 2—with no comments at all about the political intrigue or the civil conflicts. The Persian wars with the Greeks, the battles of Marathon, and the 500 Spartans at Thermopylae are all reduced to one brief statement: *"...he will arouse the whole empire against the realm of Greece."* However, according to the traditionally accepted interpretation, Daniel expends an astounding 33 verses on a period of Greek history that comprises less than 100 years. This apparent verbosity is inconsistent with Daniel and incompatible with the character of God who, though indeed lavish in His grace toward us, is nevertheless exceedingly frugal and succinct when it comes to scripture. As one Hebrew scholar noted regarding the Scriptures, "Why say something with two words when it can be said with one?"

However, the traditionalist might argue that this detailed accounting of the Greek empires is necessary because of the looming threat against the Jewish people that would be perpetrated by the evil king Antiochus Epiphanies and his desecration of the temple in Jerusalem in 167 B.C. But in making such an argument, the traditionalists would be forgetting a far more important and salient event in earlier Jewish history—the attempt of the complete genocide of the Jewish race who were scattered throughout Persia's dominion. This dastardly deed was attempted by none other than the malevolent Haman through the manipulation of Persia's King Xerxes, known in the book of Esther by his name King Ahasuerus. If, as Jerome has confidently asserted, *"Holy Scripture handles external history only so far as it is connected with God's people, Israel"*[4] , then we should expect to find some mention of this crucial episode within the first few verses of Daniel 11 — but we do not. Thus, this specious argument for the traditional interpretation falls far short of logical reasoning.

This leads to the second problem—majoring in the minutiae. Neither the Ptolemies nor the Seleucids were of any grand significance on the stage of human history. The inevitable tide of Rome was rising in the west, soon to overwhelm both

---

[4] *www.blueletterbible.com*; J.F. & B. commentary of Daniel 11:5 quoting Jerome

of them — first the Seleucid Empire and then the Ptolemies. Additionally, on the Iranian Plateau, the Parthians were approaching like a sand storm from the east to eclipse the light of democracy of the Hellenistic Seleucids. In less than 100 years, the Seleucid capital in Mesopotamia would become a battle ground between Rome and Parthia for control of the Middle East, and the land of Egypt of the Ptolemies would become a vassal state of the Roman Empire. No, the history of these hedonistic Greek overlords with their licentious boyfriends who, with the help of their tawdry wives, produced yet another generation of vile, decadent offspring amounts to little historical substance apart from its crude entertainment value. It is highly unlikely and contradictory to biblical protocol to fritter away almost an entire chapter diving into the shallow waters of these two dysfunctional families, replete with details about marital affairs, civil wars, treachery, and acts of brutality.

The third dilemma is that of the ambiguity of seemingly enigmatic phrases like *"king of the north."* The prophets were never shy about naming names and listing places: Syria, Persia, Greece, Babylon, Egypt, Elam, Edom, Arabia, Dedan, Teman, and Nineveh, *ad infinitum*. All of these locations are delineated by name in other parts of Hebrew prophetic literature. Had Daniel intended to describe Egypt (the realm of Ptolemy), he would have stated it as such, and he would not have used a mysterious term like *"king of the South."* Likewise for the *"king of the North;"* he would have called the region of the Seleucid kingdom "Babylon" or "Syria", as he does elsewhere in his writings. This is Daniel we are talking about; the one who spent the night in a lion's B&B (minus the breakfast) and had earlier rebuked King Belshazzar of Babylon to his face. Daniel would not have written mysterious code words to save his own neck—especially since the empires to which he was apparently referring would not arrive on the scene for several hundred years.

The fourth general difficulty with the traditional interpretation is the translation of the Hebrew words for "north" and "south." The Jews had no absolute terms like we have today for points on a compass nor did they conceive of imaginary lines circumscribing the globe from pole to pole. The word in Hebrew for "south" is *'negeb'*, from a root meaning "to be parched." That is, the desert. Normally, in Israel's very limited sphere of influence this would mean the desert of the Sinai to the south. But the traditional interpretation concerning chapter 11 makes the vast assumption that Daniel (who was living in Persia at the time) adjusted the term *'negeb'* to also encompass the land of Egypt, but for some inexplicable reason would not include the immeasurable *An Nafud* desert situated directly west of Persia and to the east of Israel. This endless expanse of wasteland stretches from northern Saudi Arabia north through the eastern half of Syria to the Euphrates River. Similarly, the Hebrew word for "north" is *'tsaphown'*. The 19th Century Hebrew scholar, Wilhelm Gesenius gives us the definition of *tsaphown* as: "hidden, obscure, inasmuch as the ancients regarded the north as obscure and dark; the south, on the contrary, as clear and lighted by the sun"— both literally and figuratively.[5]

Neither the sun-drenched land of Babylon nor that of Syria were obscured by clouds or hidden from the eyes of civilization since they were indeed the very cradle of ancient as well as Hellenistic civilization. Throughout the Old Testament, when the word *tsaphown* is used in relation to Israel, it is always qualified such as: *"toward the north"* or *"on the north side."* However, when it speaks of a people coming *"out*

---

[5] *Thayer's Lexicon* at blueletterbible.com

of the North," it refers to very distant places such as the realm of Magog, Gomer, or Togarmah.

At the time of his writing, Daniel was in exile in Susa, the capital city of the Persian Empire and was well east of both Syria and Babylon. In fact, the elderly Daniel had not seen his homeland since he was a young teenager. It would be odd indeed if he was calling the ruler of Babylon, Persia, and Syria the *"king of the North."* This presupposes without merit that Daniel, who was an extremely intelligent and learned man, held a narrow, Judeo-centric view of the world. Additionally, if one looks at a map, the countries of Egypt and Babylon / Persia are more west and east of Israel than they are south and north.

Fifthly, we have the premature interpretation quandary. Daniel is told by the angel Gabriel in no uncertain terms that these words are *"concealed and sealed up until the end time."*[6] How could a 4th century Christian writer like Jerome (not to mention an early 3rd century pagan like Porphyrius) possibly have the correct interpretation before the time allowed by God?

The sixth and final, broad-spectrum theological predicament is the prophetic tunnel vision that is ascribed to the Hebrew prophets. This initiates that pesky hurdle of the gap in time, the 2,250 year (and counting) Royal Gorge into which the river of time disappears between the last viable Ptolemaic verse—verse 35—and the seemingly obvious transition (as interpreted by today's experts) in the very next verse into the end times and the rise of the anti-Christ. The implausible explanation we are given here (initially by Jerome and oft repeated) is that the Hebrew prophets could see into the future before and during the first and second advents of Christ, but could not see the time in between, that is during the church age. For some inexplicable reason they were not allowed to see into the future unless it directly affected the nation of Israel. There is no scripture to support this assumption, and as I will soon delineate, scripture itself contradicts this fallacy. This is a supposition without merit, a theory without validity.

This conjecture that has gone unchallenged for two millennia has formed the foundation for general Old Testament prophecy interpretation and has been accepted, seemingly without question. This has led to the allegorical construction of an odd little cottage composed from a mere handful of viable prophetic interpretations founded upon a bed of sand. In contrast, God desires that you discover that there is a prophetic edifice of Smithsonian proportions, built upon a foundation of granite bedrock just waiting to be marveled at and explored.

PART 3—Problems of a historical nature:

As I mentioned in the introduction, there are 108 specific events that are foretold by Daniel concerning the future unfolding of history from verses 2 through 38 of chapter 11. In the Appendix, I list all of these events in tabular form with special attention given to commentaries by Dr. John F. Walvoord of *Dallas Theological Seminary* and the 17th century work by Jameison, Fauset & Brown. The commentaries that are available for review on-line[7] or in book form (and which I have read either in part or in their entirety) are:

---

[6] Daniel 12:9
[7] *www.blueletterbible.org*

- Jerome (342 A.D.)—a quick read of his work verifies that his commentary is the basis for all others.
- Sir Isaac Newton (1704)—Though Sir Isaac's works on differential and integral calculus are truly enlightening and his discovery of the laws of planetary motion are equally God-inspired, when it comes to his Biblical commentary I find that he waxes long amongst rambling tributaries of irrelevant history.
- Matthew Henry (1714)—Henry approaches Daniel 11 from the point of view of a teacher and so he does go into some detail. However, he totally ignores the portions of history that do not fit the traditional interpretation.
- Jameison, Fauset & Brown (1871) — I used their commentary as a baseline, for they go into more explanation and detail than does Henry. Where Henry ignores some of the details, J.F. & B. at least attempted to address more of them. Quoting Charles Spurgeon: *"It (J.F. & B.) is to some extent a compilation and condensation of other men's thoughts, but it is sufficiently original to claim a place in every minister's library..."*[8]
- John F. Walvoord (1971)—also uses a teacher-like approach to the prophecy. Though he does disagree with J.F. & B. in minor places, he strongly maintains the traditional interpretation for Daniel 11 as published in his work, *Daniel—the Key to Prophetic Revelation* (1971, *Moody Bible Institute*). His works are endorsed by noted radio personality, Pastor Chuck Swindol.
- Pastor Chuck Smith (2000)—also nearly identical to Pastor Smith are his associates, Steve Guzick and Pastor John Corson. Smith and Corson approach the prophecy primarily from a preacher / exhorter viewpoint while Guzick has just a bit more of the critical, teacher mentality. Much like Sir Isaac Newton, who swims about in the swirling eddies of the flow of history, the three *Calvary Chapel* pastors similarly tend to wax eloquent in their somewhat unrelated scriptural exhortations. The problem with the exhortation style commentaries of all three is that like Henry, there is the uniform tendency to look right through those historical or prophetical events that do not fit their point of view –a fact which is easily hidden in the abundance of words, albeit unintentionally no doubt.

For the sake of readability, I will not go into all of the historical inaccuracies of the traditional interpretation at this point in the book but will save that for the appendix. At this point I will concentrate on a few of the more blatant examples as evidence of the historical fallacy of the traditional interpretation.

Right out of the starting gate, the traditional interpretation makes a fundamental fatal flaw that causes it to proceed down the wrong path. Though this particular error has more to do with grammar than it does with history, it is critical for this issue to be addressed for a proper understanding of the remainder of the chapter.

3. And a mighty king will arise, (this is Alexander the Great) and he will rule with great authority and do as he pleases. 4. But as soon as he has arisen, his kingdom will be broken up and parceled out toward the four winds of heaven, though not to his descendants, nor according to his authority which he wielded; for his sovereignty will be uprooted and given to others besides these.[9]

---

[8] ibid

The error here is made by trying to incorrectly identify the final word, *"these"*, as referring to the children of Alexander. The NASB, in fact, states this in the footnotes, *"i.e. his descendants."* This is an obvious instance of garment alteration by the interpreting tailor. In making this initial error, the traditionalist tailors proceed to force-fit the remainder of the garment (the lingering 100 years of Greek history) onto the wrong body (the prophecy). The proper grammar should read:

4. But as soon as he has arisen, his kingdom will be broken up and parceled out toward the four winds of heaven (though not to his descendants, nor according to his authority which he wielded) for his sovereignty will be uprooted and given to others besides these.

Then, if we remove the parenthetical phrase, the meaning becomes obvious:
4. But as soon as he has arisen, his kingdom will be broken up and parceled out toward the four winds of heaven (...) for his sovereignty will be uprooted and given to others besides these.

Period! No footnote is needed for explanation. The proper identification of *"these"* in the sentence is an obvious reference to Alexander's four Generals and not to his offspring: *"...for his sovereignty will be uprooted and given to others besides these [generals]."* The fact that Alexander's children will not inherit the kingdom is an "aside" fact of reference only and is not germane to the rest of the prophecy. So here at the end of verse 4, the true interpretation, which will be expounded upon shortly, will take the road less traveled and depart from the history of the inconsequential and crumbling Greek empire.

Now however, for the sake of argument, let's pretend that the grammar that is inferred in the traditional interpretation is correct and continue with the cross-examination of some historical facts.

Fact # I

5. Then the king of the South will grow strong, along with one of his princes who will gain ascendancy over him...

Here, J.F. & B. drag another family member into the squabble, Ptolemy Lagus. He was the father of Ptolemy Soter and the possible (though the latest historical facts deem it unlikely) father of another illegitimate son Seleucus Nicator. J.F. & B. want the verse to be read thus:

5. Then the king of the South [Ptolemy Soter—the son] will grow strong, along with one of his [Ptolemy Lagus—the father] princes [that is Seleucus Nicator—the illegitimate son] who will gain ascendancy over him [Ptolemy Lagus]...

In order to make this pretzel-interpretation work, one has to totally ignore a major figure in Greek history— Alexander the Great! Lagus had been a man of some im-

---
[9] Daniel 11:3

portance during the reign of Alexander's father, Phillip of Macedonia, but all of this became moot with the conquests of Alexander and his conquering generals who included Ptolemy Soter and Seleucus Nicator. Seleucus Nicator was satrap (governor) in his own right and was never a *"prince"* under the authority of Lagus or of Soter.

Fact # II

5…his domain will be a vast dominion indeed.

By superlative implication, this person, whoever he may be, will have a dominion that even surpasses that of Alexander the Great. Yet none of the commentators gives a reasonable explanation of this portion of scripture. J.F. & B. apply this portion to Seleucus Nicator on the one hand while admitting that his dominion is less than Alexander's on the other hand. Most commentators ignore this portion entirely and offer no explanation. The silence is deafening.

Fact # III

14. Now in those times many will rise up against the king of the South; the violent ones (or robbers) among your people will also lift themselves up in order to fulfill the vision, but they will stumble.

The meaning here could not be any clearer. Violent Jews (Daniel's people) will rise up in the conscious hope of fulfilling some vision or dream through unscrupulous or even violent means—yet they will not be successful in this endeavor. However, J.F. & B. (and Walvoord et. al) spin this to read:

"Those turbulent Jews unconsciously shall help to fulfill the purpose of God, as to the trials which await Judea; according to this vision…Though helping to fulfill the vision, they shall fail in their aim, of making Judea independent."[10]

So historically, here is what happened and how this verse is twisted by J.F. & B. to fit history:
- Some Jews wanted to rebel against Ptolemy of Egypt. So they supported Antiochus of the Seleucid kingdom in Syria in his battles against the Ptolemy kingdom in the south.
- The Seleucid kingdom was victorious in the battle and so Judea was transferred to the domain of the Seleucids in the north. Thus these Jews were successful. They did not *"stumble"* in fulfilling their short-term vision for Judea.
- Since the prophecy states unequivocally that *"they will stumble"*, J.F. & B. must change something. Aha! It was God's vision of punishment upon Judea that these Jews were manipulated by God into fulfilling—not their own vision.
- So:
  - They were successful in fulfilling God's long-term vision of punishment (even though God is not mentioned in the verse)

---

[10] www.blueletterbible.com ; J.F. & B. commentary on Daniel 11

- And they were successful in fulfilling their own short-term vision (which according to J.F. & B. is not suggested in the verse)
- But they were not successful in fulfilling their own long-term vision of independence (even though no such additional vision was mentioned in the verse).

Yes. It's all becoming clearer now.

Fact # IV

20. Then in his place one will arise…yet within a few days he will be shattered, though neither in anger nor in battle.

The meaning here is very clear—someone dies. The "someone", according to J.F. & B., is Seleucus Philopater of Syria who was poisoned by his own viceroy, Heliodorus who wanted the throne for himself. Yes…it was murder most foul! So according to J.F. & B. et.al, Heliodorus was not "angry" when he murdered his master—he may have even been smiling. So J.F. & B. believe that cold calculating murder is a fulfillment of this prophecy.

I strongly disagree.

Fact # V

15. Then the king of the North will come, cast up a siege mound, and capture a well-fortified city;

All of the commentators define this as the Battle of Paneas (198 B.C.), located at the headwaters of the Jordan River. The problems with the interpretation here are inexcusably transparent.
- The Battle of Paneas was out on the open plain between two cavalry forces
- There was no *"siege mound"*
- There was no *"well-fortified city"*

When the defeat of the forces of Egypt was inevitable, Ptolemy's General Scopus made a hasty retreat to the port city of Sidon. It was a two to three day's journey at least, but the battle was well over by the time he reached sanctuary. The Seleucid army—not wanting any more casualties or destruction within a city that, due to their victory at Paneas, was now within their realm— surrounded the city until the threat of starvation forced those within the city to deliver Scopus to his captors. There was no siege mound. Nor did those within the city shoot arrows or launch attacks against the Seleucid army garrisoned outside the walls. It was merely a waiting game with a relatively short duration.

Fact # VI

21. And in his place a despicable person will arise, on whom the honor of kingship has not been conferred, but he will come in a time of tranquility and seize the kingdom by intrigue (or flatteries).

This, according to the traditional commentaries, would be the infamous Antiochus Epiphanies, who would later sacrifice a pig upon the altar in the temple at Jerusalem and kill many of the Jews.
- Was he *"despicable?"* Most certainly.
- But, in contrast to the scripture verse, was the honor of kingship legitimately conferred upon him? Yes, it was.
- And did his rise to the position as king of the Seleucids eclipse that of any of the other scoundrels? No.
- Was it a *"time of tranquility?"* That's debatable.

Historically, here is the short story. Rome was becoming increasingly annoyed with this constant warfare between the Seleucids and the Roman vassal state of the Ptolemy kingdom of Egypt. Rome had forced Seleucus Philopater (the one who was soon to be gleefully poisoned) to a peace treaty. To assure compliance with the terms, Rome kept Philopater's eldest son, Demetrius, under house arrest in Rome under penalty of death should his father fail to keep the terms of the treaty. After Heliodorus poisoned Philopater, the rightful heir was Philopater's younger son who was only a boy. Antiochus Epiphanies, who was Philopater's brother, seized the opportunity and the throne for himself. Walvoord and others claim that Epiphanies *"seized the throne rather than obtaining it honorably,"* as if this act was something novel. Here is a brief synopsis of this sordid family history:
- Seleucus Nicator I murdered the regent Perdiccas in order to secure his portion of Alexander's empire.
- Cassander had the 13-year-old son of Alexander the Great assassinated, along with his mother, in order to secure the Greek homeland.
- Antiochus I Soter (son and successor to Seleucus Nicator I) was obliged to have his own flesh and blood, his eldest son, executed on charges of rebellion.
- Antiochus I Soter (of the Seleucid kingdom) left the empire to his second son, Antiochus II Theos. This is the same one that divorced his wife Laodice to marry Bernice of the Ptolemy kingdom. He lost the empire when he and his wife Bernice were murdered by his "ex"—Laodice. "Hell hath no fury…" as the saying goes.
- Laodice installed her own son, Seleucus II Callinicus on the throne. He was succeeded by his eldest son, Seleucus III Ceraunus.
- Seleucus III Ceraunus, after three years of rule, was murdered by his own army leaving the empire to his younger brother, Antiochus III the Great.
- Antiochus III was succeeded by his son Seleucus IV Philopater who was murdered by his minister, Heliodorus. The true heir to the throne was being held as a hostage by the Romans as a condition of the Treaty of Apamea.
- Antiochus Epiphanies was Philopater's younger brother and also a son to Antiochus III.

The fact that Epiphanies decided that he should rule rather than his young nephew who was but a child is nothing out of the ordinary in the lineage or heritage of this ruthless and dysfunctional family. Unlike many before him, he didn't even have to murder someone to obtain the throne. On the "despicable-o-meter" it is hard to label Epiphanies as "more despicable" than the rest of the family. One can only imagine the peace and joyous celebrations of the family reunions!

Fact # VII

The final historical inaccuracies that strain credulity to the breaking point are found in the interpretation of verses 23 through 26. According to the narrative in Daniel, the battles continue in succession with the repeat of the chronologically conjunctive phrases, *"...and he will... [do this]...and after he will [do that]..."* The problem for the traditionalists is that they have run out of historical battles! Following the flow of their interpretation leads them to the end of the Syrian Wars around verse 22, yet more battles are enumerated in the prophecy. What to do? According to J.F. & B. and the others, the angel Gabriel started repeating himself.

Of verse 25 J.F. & B. state:
"25. A fuller detail of what was summarily stated in verses 22-24."[11]

Again regarding verse 29 J.F. & B. state:
"...the time spoken of in Dan 11:27."[12]

And again of verse 40 they state:
"This Dan 11:40, therefore, may be a recapitulation summing up the facts of the first expedition to Egypt (171-170 B.C.), in Dan 11:22, 25"[13]

There were six major campaigns of the Syrian Wars between the Seleucid kingdom and the Ptolemy kingdom interspersed within a time frame of approximately 100 years. The first three campaigns are apparently not worth mentioning according to the traditional interpretation yet the last one is apparently worth repeating three times. To infer that Gabriel later remembers something that he had forgotten to mention earlier is unimaginable and humorous. I shall have to ask Gabriel about this "senior moment" when I see him in heaven.

PART 4—In conclusion of the traditional iterpretation:

In the Appendix, I submit a grading system for the different commentators. Since I expound upon it in detail there, I will merely state here that none of the commentators who hold to the traditional interpretation score higher than a failing grade of 59% accuracy—and that is being generous in my opinion. As a Christian who believes in the inspired, infallible Word of God, I find an interpretation that is correct only 59% of the time to be wholly intolerable. Either the prophecy is incorrect (which it can't be) or the interpretation is unacceptable and objectionable (though a score of 59% is far better than the average for a Nostradamus quatrain). To disregard specific details and phrases of a prophecy because it doesn't seem to fit the traditional interpretation could be construed as a lack of objectivity by outside critics. Worse, it leaves Christians open to justifiable criticism by secularists by playing fast and loose with writings that we hold as sacred and infallible.

---

[11] www.blueletterbible.com ; J.F. & B. commentary on Daniel 11
[12] ibid
[13] ibid

Were I to speculate as to the willingness to accept this Porphyrius/Jerome interpretation for so long of a time, it is probably due to the singular, apparent fulfillment in verse 31 of the *"...abomination of desolation..."* as perpetrated by Antiochus Epiphanies in 167 BC. But the truth of the matter was that the pagan cultures during that era had made Jewish sanctuary desolation almost as common as cow-tipping in Nebraska.
• In 167 BC, Antiochus Epiphanies sacrificed a pig upon the temple altar.
• In 63 BC, General Pompey of Rome desecrated the temple in Jerusalem by murdering the priests within the Holy of Holies itself, a far worse crime than that which was perpetrated by Epiphanies.
• In 70 AD, General Titus destroyed Jerusalem and looted and burned the temple.
• In 135 AD, Emperor Hadrian had the remaining portions of Jerusalem and the temple razed to the ground in fulfillment of Jesus' prophecy in Matthew 24 that, *"...not one stone shall be left upon another."*

However, in order for these 38 verses in Daniel to have a viable, objective, interpretation, it must be supported throughout the entire prophecy and not just revolve around one verse vis-à-vis temple desecration.

PART 5—A preface to the true interpretation:

I now submit for the reader's consideration, enjoyment, and wonder a correct interpretation of the prophecy in Daniel chapter 11. This interpretation removes all of the problems of a general nature that are prevalent in the traditional interpretation. This interpretation:
• Removes the time-scale problem—we do not see 36 verses comprising a mere century of Hellenistic history. Daniel's vision remains generally consistent with the *centuries per verse,* time-scale with which he begins in verse two. The 36 verses from 2 through 38 cover 2,250 years of history from the time of Daniel to the present day. The events generally break up into intervals spanning centuries of relative quiet, punctuated by wars and conflicts.
• Removes the gap in time and prophecy flows continuously in conjunction with history upon the River of Time.
• Enlightens the reader with the understanding that Daniel's prophecy was majoring in the professional league—not the minors. Most readers, not just historians and scholars, will at least be acquainted with the characters and events that are named in this interpretation. These are the major players upon the drama of human history.
• Reveals that the prophecy is no longer *"concealed and sealed up until the end time,"* because we are in the end time.
• Explains Daniel's mysterious language and ambiguity. The reason that Daniel uses the phrase *"king of the North"* or *"king of the South"* is NOT because he is purposefully trying to be enigmatic but precisely because the centers of power of the two empires change throughout the centuries. The phrases do not refer to any one country or to any one ethnicity but rather to entire continental and multi-continental regions. The phrase *"king of the North"* refers to that current emperor that becomes preeminent among all the realms of the northern kingdoms at that particular time in history—so too with the term for the south, again, regardless of ethnicity.

- Reveals that the terms for "north" and "south" are better interpreted as consistent with their true meanings. The word *tsaphown* is not Syria, but the obscure, clouded, and hidden region of Europe. The region inhabited by the sons of Japheth, the white-skin races and their descendants (Gaul, Celt, Germanic, Goths, Rus, & Visigoths). Likewise the word *negeb* is not limited to Egypt alone but to the sun-drenched, parched, desert region of the entire Middle East and North Africa inhabited predominantly by the sons of Shem (Arabs, Jews, Turks as well as the non-Semitic Persians, Berbers and Syrians).

For what Daniel is foreseeing are not skirmishes and inconsequential Hellenistic civil wars but rather the clash of two entire civilizations. Consistent with the Almighty God who is the Author of all of history and controls the destiny of nations, Daniel foresees a confrontation with multiple collisions—a confrontation between the northern empires of Christian Europe and the southern caliphates of the Islamic Middle East! The overriding presumption of prophetic tunnel vision (i.e. being unable to see into the time of the Church Age) is shown to be irrelevant and is dismissed. And I promise the reader that every specific detail, whether stated or implied in the scriptures, is addressed and elaborated upon in light of historical events. Now, please join me as we marvel together and explore but one room in the Smithsonian of Prophecy...

THE CONFLICT BEGINS

King of the North

King of the South

DANIEL, CHAPTER 11:

3. And a mighty king [Alexander the Great] *will arise, and he will rule with great authority and do as he pleases. 4. But as soon as he has arisen...*

As previously explained, Alexander died soon after he had completed his conquests. He had very little time to enjoy the fruits of his labor and did not even live long enough to see the birth of his son and heir, Alexander IV.

4...his kingdom will be broken up and parceled out toward the four winds of the heavens (alt. trans NASB.), though not to his own descendants...

As other commentators have correctly written, Alexander's legitimate heir, Alexander IV was assassinated at the age of 13 subsequent to the division of the empire between four of Alexander's generals, Seleucus Nicator, Ptolemy Soter, Lysimachus, and Cassander. These quickly decreased to three contenders within the first generation with the conquest of Thrace (parts of Turkey, Bulgaria and Greece)—that was initially held by Lysimachus—to Seleucus Nicator.

4...nor according to his authority which he wielded...

None of his generals would attain to Alexander's level of success. They were inferior in territory and in rule.

4...for his kingdom shall be plucked up, even for others besides these. (HNV)

Here Daniel completes his forecast of the Hellenistic rulers of the Ptolemies and the Seleucids. For having previously said, *"...his kingdom will be broken up and parceled out..."* he plainly states here that even those who carved out portions of the kingdom for themselves will not keep their portions but they will be

DANIEL, CHAPTER 11:3-4

3. And a mighty king will arise, and he will rule with great authority and do as he pleases. 4. But as soon as he has arisen his kingdom will be broken up and parceled out toward the four winds of the heavens, though not to his own descendants nor according to his authority which he wielded for his kingdom shall be plucked up, even for others besides these.

Alexander the Great (356-323 BC)

Ptolemy I Soter and his wife Eurydice

given *"...even for others besides these."* He carefully words this in the imperfect aspect indicating that it is not immediate—but will soon happen nevertheless. However, we will soon see that there is yet one, last Ptolemaic ruler to be mentioned— *"the daughter of the king of the south."*

{Biblical Hebrew had only two aspects (not tenses). The perfect aspect was used for completed actions, and generally implies past time. The imperfect aspect was used for uncompleted actions, and thus could imply present and/or future time. Most prophecy is written in the *prophetic perfect* aspect. That is, it is written as if it were a completed action unless the prophet is trying to describe an event that occurs chronologically in the future from the event just described—db}

{ Historical Timeline—Rome acquired a great deal of its territory in the 1st and 2nd centuries BC through treaty rather than through conquest. Even as Greece sought to expand its empire against Rome, Greek rivals of the Antigonoid dynasty came to Rome's aid.
- 196 BC— Macedon succumbed to the Roman legions.
- 134 BC— Rome conquers Spain
- 133 BC— Rome had created 6 independent provinces: Sicily, Sardinia, the two Spains, Macedon, and Africa.

Civil war erupted in Rome in the late 80's. Roman General and Consul, Lucius Sulla called upon his forces to march on Rome herself. Sulla became dictator. Republican procedures were suspended and his enemies were hunted down and killed, their property confiscated, and their children disenfranchised. Once in command of the city of Rome, he disbanded his army and restored control to the Senate. He resigned and retired by 78 BC. Three Roman generals arose to prominence following this time:
- Pompey—he became the son-in-law of Sulla and later the son-in-law of Julius Caesar. Undefeated in every battle, he achieved rock-star status with the public. He defeated the Greek Seleucids and secured Syria and Judea where he entered the Holy of Holies in Jerusalem and slew the priests in 63 BC.
- Crassus—defeated the slave rebellion led by Spartacus and led an army against the Parthians c. 55 BC. He was one of the wealthiest men in history with a combined fortune equivalent to $170 billion in today's dollars. There was no love lost between him and Pompey.
- Julius Caesar—the victorious conqueror of Gaul (France & Germany). He invaded Britain in 55 BC. Crassus and Caesar were close friends—Pompey was his respected rival. The Roman historian Suetonius recorded how Caesar was hidden by friends during the aforementioned purges of General Sulla, who was bent on killing him. Sulla believed, and was proven accurate by history, that Caesar had too much ambition and was a danger to the republic. After multiple acquaintances and friends of the aristocracy interceded with Sulla on Caesar's behalf, *"[Sulla] at last gave way and cried, either by divine inspiration or a shrewd forecast: 'Have your way and take him; only bear in mind that the man you are so eager to save will one day deal the death blow to the cause of the aristocracy'"*[14]

Political alliances during this time were nothing if not treacherous. Neither blood-ties nor friendships would prevail against the lust for power.

---

[14] http://penelope.uchicago.edu/Thayer/E/Roman/Texts/Suetonius/12Caesars/Julius*.html

- 59 BC—Pompey, Crassus, and Caesar form the *First Triumvirate*, controlling all of Rome's legions and throwing around their weight in the Senate.
- 53 BC— Crassus is killed in Syria in a battle with Parthia. Friction between Pompey and Caesar becomes openly hostile.
- 51 BC—Ptolemy XII Aulets, the Hellenistic ruler of Rome's vassal state of Egypt, dies. The Roman Senate appoints Pompey as legal guardian of Cleopatra VII (who will soon write her own chapter in history) and her two younger brothers, Ptolemy XIII and Ptolemy XIV until they come of age to rule on their own. **This Senate appointment of Pompey becomes very important in fulfillment of Daniel's prophecy as will shortly be described.**
- 49 BC—Back in Rome, Pompey and the Senate openly condemn Julius Caesar. In a brazen show of force, rather than succumb to their justice, Caesar violates Roman law by leading one of his legions across the Rubicon River, invading the city of Rome itself and igniting a civil war. Pompey and the Senate flee the city. After securing the city, Caesar leaves Rome in control of his right-hand man, Mark Antony, to pursue Pompey, having never actually ruled in Rome itself.
- 48 BC—After Pompey's forces are twice defeated by Caesar's, Pompey sails about the Mediterranean for 40 days fleeing from Caesar and eventually deciding in September to head toward Egypt to seek asylum with the young Ptolemies whom he had protected and reared. Ptolemy the XIII, now but a young teenager, greets him at the dock in Alexandria, where upon his signal, General Pompey is murdered and decapitated on the spot in order to curry favor with Caesar. Arriving shortly thereafter with the might of his legions, Caesar is aghast as he is presented with the head of his old friend and rival. Escorted by two legions and 800 cavalry, Caesar enters the city as a conqueror, sets himself upon the Egyptian throne and begins dispensing orders. Cleopatra (who was in hiding for her life from her younger brother) has herself smuggled into Caesar's apartment that night; the two become lovers and she secures her place upon the throne of Egypt.
- 47 BC—After a three month civil war (omitting the details here), Caesar secures the Egyptian throne for Cleopatra, disposes of the young upstart Ptolemy XIII, and sets himself upon the throne of Egypt where he rules with his new queen, Cleopatra, for the next 3 years. Though he never officially takes the title of Pharaoh for himself, there can be little doubt that Caesar was the true power behind the throne:

"Caesar was Egypt's Master."[15]

He settles in Alexandria, and in April he and Cleopatra embark upon a two month lover's voyage up the Nile upon her luxurious pleasure barge escorted by a flotilla of 40 ships. In June of 47, Cleopatra gives birth to Caesar's son, Caesarion. Over the next year, Caesar engages and triumphs in several military campaigns—mostly in North Africa. But, was it the empire of Rome that he was expanding—or Egypt's?}

5. Then the king of the South will grow strong (imperfect aspect—present-to-future; that is—a process)...

Julius Caesar becomes this *"king of the South"* of whom Daniel speaks. Over the next 3 years he first rules Egypt and then the Roman Empire, not from Rome, but

---

[15] Cleopatra—the Life and Death of a Pharaoh; Edith Flamarion; Discoveries/Abrams, New York

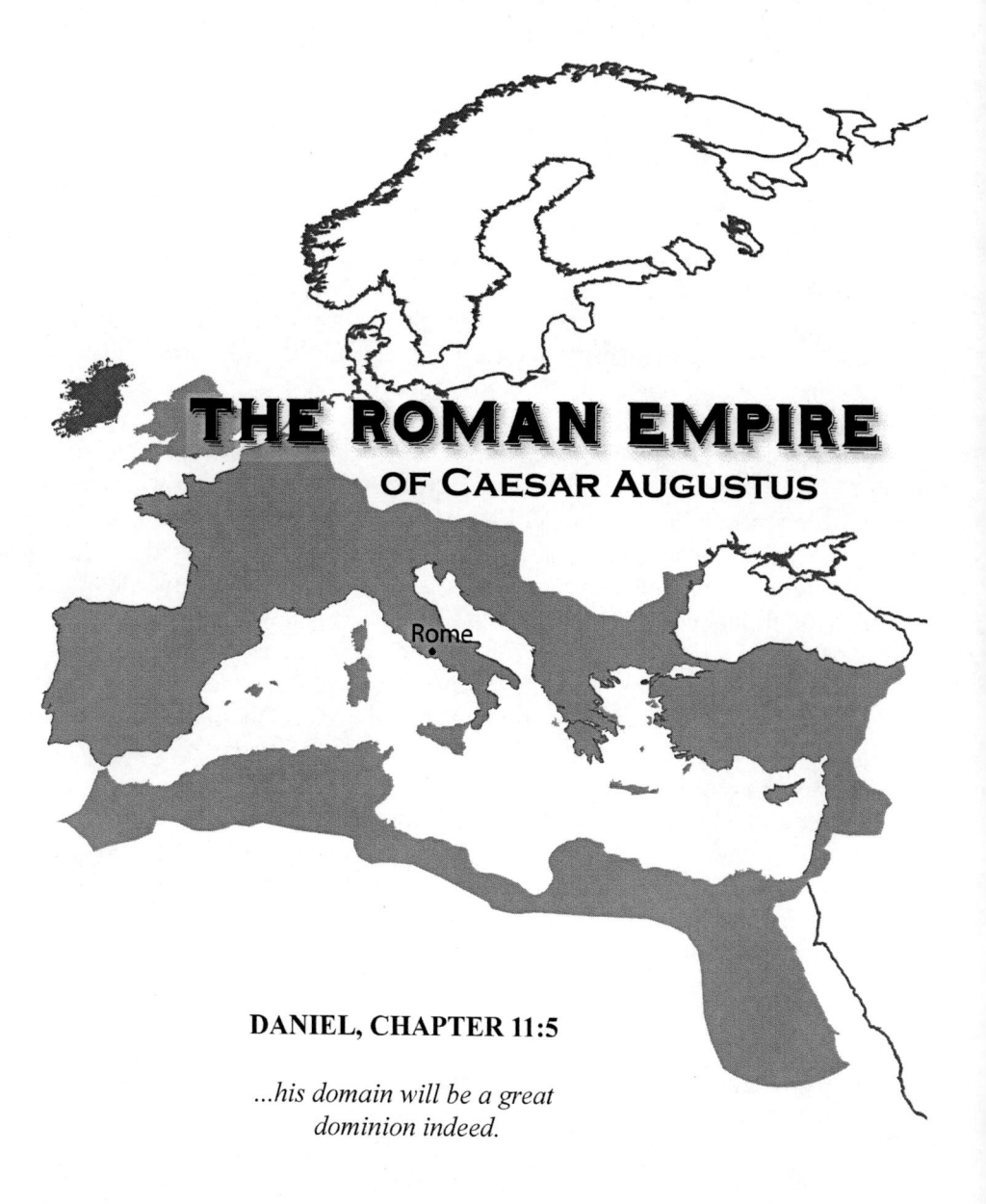

THE ROMAN EMPIRE
OF CAESAR AUGUSTUS

Rome

DANIEL, CHAPTER 11:5

...his domain will be a great dominion indeed.

primarily from Alexandria, Egypt. He returns to Rome only for brief visits and then only to be honored. (Now be honest, Caesar is a 52-year-old pagan, and he is 2 weeks out from Rome. An attractive, intelligent, sophisticated, 21-year-old woman who is wealthy beyond belief throws herself at his feet—her only desire is to make him happy. Where do you think he spent most of his time?) Caesar turned down the initial, lifetime dictatorship offered by the Senate, preferring instead the title of "First Citizen". He is elected in absentia as exclusive Consul of the Senate in 46 BC, and in 45 BC he is given many honors and a ten-year dictatorship—only 5 months before his assassination.

{ Historical Timeline—44 BC—Caesar returns to Rome and is assassinated on the Ides of March by the Senate, led by his one-time friend Marcus Brutus. Whatever chances the Republic had of survival vanished in the aftermath of the assassination. In one corner: Brutus, Cassius, and Cicero, the great orator, were claiming to carry the torch for the Republic. In the other corner: Caesar's lieutenant Marc Antony and the dictator's grand-nephew, Octavian, who joined forces in 43 BC. Brutus, Cassius, and Cicero were all slain and the Octavian-Antony forces ruled the day. }

5...but one of his princes shall be stronger than he and shall rule... (imperfect aspect again, denoting a process)...his domain will be a great (vast) dominion indeed. (ESV)
Caesar had two *"princes"* as Daniel states: his blood-son with Cleopatra, named Caesarion; and his grand-nephew and adopted son, Octavian, whom he made his sole heir in 45 BC. Octavian was indeed to become stronger in the not too distant future. Proclaiming himself as *Caesar Augustus*, his empire would eventually stretch from Babylon to

DANIEL, CHAPTER 11:5

5. Then the king of the south will grow strong but one of his princes shall be stronger than he and shall rule...his domain will be a great dominion indeed.

Julius Caesar
"...the king of the south will grow strong."

Caesar Augustus
"but one of his princes shall be stronger than he and shall rule..."

Britain and to the Pillars of Hercules in North Africa—*"...a vast dominion indeed."* and far greater than the dominion of Alexander the Great.

6. And in the end of years they shall join themselves together (lit. "couple themselves")...
The remainder of the verse implies who is joining themselves together—*"the daughter [maiden, young woman*[16]*] of the king of the South"* with someone from *"the North"*—but not the king. The very absence of the term indicates its importance. At this point, Daniel just refers to them as *"they."* With Julius Caesar gone, Marc Antony, the co-ruler of the North with Octavian, joins himself (on every level) to Caesar's *"young woman,"* Cleopatra, and that not without her encouragement. Cleopatra, on the other hand, has now become one of the most powerful women in history. Was Daniel's term *"...in the end of years..."* a reference to the couple's impending demise? Or were his words foretelling the countdown of years B.C. and the coming of the Messiah in less than 35 years? (Daniel had previously prophesied the exact date of Messiah in chapter 9:25, 26.)

{ <u>Historical Timeline</u>—Antony and Octavian's mutual allegiance was slim at best and punctuated by quarrels and friction. Antony's tendency to give away large chunks of Rome's real estate (Crete, Syria, Judea, and Mesopotamia) as gifts to his new girlfriend did little to help the situation. But when Antony divorced Octavia, his wife of many years and the sister of Octavian, war broke out again. Octavian routed the eastern forces of Antony and his consort Cleopatra in 31 BC. The navy battle at Actium was a minor skirmish militarily, but decisively made Octavian the undisputed ruler of the Mediterranean world. Octavian would change his name to Caesar Augustus in 27 BC, and in a series of steps, would become the absolute dictator of the Roman Empire. }

6...for the young woman [Cleopatra] of the king of the South [Julius Caesar] will come to the king of the North [Octavian] to carry out an equitable agreement. But she will not retain her position of power...
Here, and not without reason, is the first mention of the "king of the North." After the defeat of his navy at Actium, Antony fled to Cleopatra and committed suicide, thus leaving Octavian as the singular, king of the North. Ever the brazen optimist, Cleopatra sails to Rome in a third endeavor at keeping her expansive empire intact, but Octavian would have none of it. Antony is beneath contempt to Octavian, and Cleopatra is to be paraded as a slave through the streets of Rome, Cairo, and Damascus as a trophy before being exiled or executed—just as she had done three years prior to her younger sister Arsinoë.

6...nor will he [Marc Antony] remain with his power...
6... but she will be given up...
Cleopatra uses an asp, or Egyptian cobra to commit suicide, thus securing her dying wish not to be forgotten.

---

[16] Gesenius states the Hebrew word can be equally translated as: *daughter, maiden,* or *young woman*. Sometimes it is also used as a polite term. Cleopatra was after all Caesar's *"young woman"* and young-enough to be his daughter.

6...along with those who brought her in... that is, her royal handmaidens, who, according to the Roman historian Plutarch, were also found dead or dying from apparent snake bite.[17]

6...and he who became a father to her (HNV)... that is, General Pompey, her legal guardian and protector.[18]

6...as well as he who supported her during those times. Julius Caesar—assassinated on the Ides of March.

Daniel is saying here that pretty much everyone associated with Cleopatra will end up being murdered. This of course does happen:
• During the beginnings of her reign with Caesar, Cleopatra had her two brothers and her sister executed.
• Pompey was murdered.
• Julius Caesar was assassinated.
• Octavian had Caesarion executed when he was but a boy.
• Antony chose suicide over execution.
• Antony and Cleopatra had three children, the two boys were executed as children but the one daughter did grow up to marry Octavian's friend, King Juba II of Numidia (North Africa). Their only son, Ptolemy, became King of Mauretania (now Morocco) and was later invited to Rome in 40 AD, to be honored by Emperor Caligula. However, as he entered the amphitheater to resounding applause for wearing a purple cloak, Caligula, in a fit of envy had him murdered.

{ Historical Timeline—history truly becomes *His Story*, as God robes himself in human flesh by being immaculately conceived in a young virgin maiden in

DANIEL, CHAPTER 11:6

6. And in the end of years they shall join themselves together for the young woman of the king of the South will come to the king of the North to carry out an equitable agreement. But she will not retain her position of power...nor will he remain with his power... but she will be given up along with those who brought her in and he who became a father to her as well as he who supported her during those times.

Cleopatra
"the young woman of the king of the South."

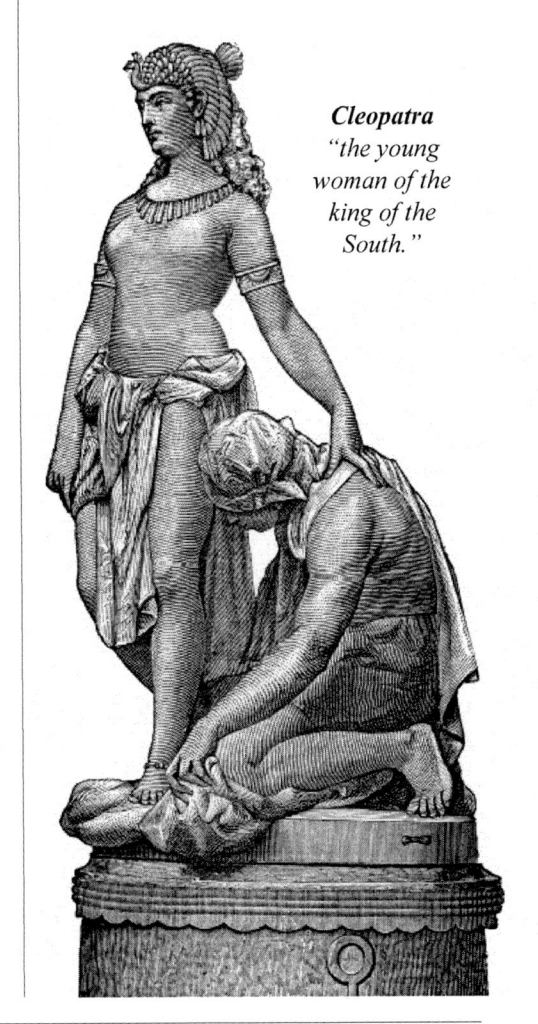

[17] Plutarch, Parallel Lives, LXXXV 2-3 (Life of Antony)
[18] http://www.egyptologyonline.com/cleopatra.htm

the province of Judea of the Empire of Rome. *"Now it came about in those days that a decree went out from Caesar Augustus, that a census be taken of all the inhabited earth…And Joseph also went up from Galilee, from the city of Nazareth…along with Mary, who was engaged to him, and was with child."*[19]
• ~33 AD—Jesus Christ is crucified and raised from the dead.
• 33 AD-90 AD—Christ appoints His Apostles to spread the Gospel before His ascension into heaven. The fledgling church grows under the teachings of the Apostles. Rome goes through a series of emperors and the Church endures persecution under several of them.
• 70 AD—Following a Jewish rebellion, the Romans burn the Temple in Jerusalem and destroy the city. The rebels at Masada commit group suicide prior to being overrun.
• 135 AD—Jerusalem is razed to the ground by the Romans.
• 224 AD—The Sassanid Empire rises on the Iranian plateau—defeating the Parthians.
• 286 AD—Unable to effectively govern the vast empire, Rome is split up into the East and West kingdoms under Emperor Diocletian.
• 313 AD—The pagan Emperor Constantine converts to Christianity, making it the official religion of the Roman Empire. He builds a new capital city for Rome, naming it *Constantinople*, situated on the mouth of the Black Sea.
• 410 AD—Here begins the ascent of the time of the Barbarians, as the Western Roman Empire finally succumbs, and Rome, the "eternal city", is invaded by Alaric I of the Visigoths. Europe falls into a dark-age, with assorted tribes of Franks, Angles, Saxons, Gauls, Goths, Visigoths, Lombardi, Huns, and Britons vying for dominance over various regions.
• 565 AD—The Byzantine Empire (the region of Turkey or Asia Minor which will always be part of the *"South"* Empire) is in conflict with the Sassanid Empire, also of the south. The Byzantines maintain a tenuous hold on Palestine, Egypt, and North Africa during the time of their greatest expansion.
• 570 AD—Mohammed is born in Mecca of the Hejaz on the Arabian Peninsula. His religion, united with war and violence, quickly spreads throughout all Arabia. Arab Christians living in the Levant (Syria and Israel) are killed or forced to convert during the Muslim *Wars of Apostasy*.
• 660 AD—after the death of Mohammed, one tribe emerges triumphant forming the Umayyad Caliphate. Damascus, Syria, is made their capital as Islam spreads to the borders of India and Kazakhstan in the east, defeating the Sassanid Empire, and across North Africa in the west. The Umayyad Caliphate and the Byzantine Empire maintain a stalemate resulting in Byzantium acting as a buffer between Europe and the Middle East.

Though the prophets Isaiah and Jeremiah do foresee conflicts within the Middle East itself and foretell the coming of *Dar al Islam*, Daniel does not. This is because there is little warfare and little interaction between the *"North"* (where there are no empires) and the *"South"* for over 600 years—but that is soon to change…}

---

[19] Luke 2:1,4, and 5

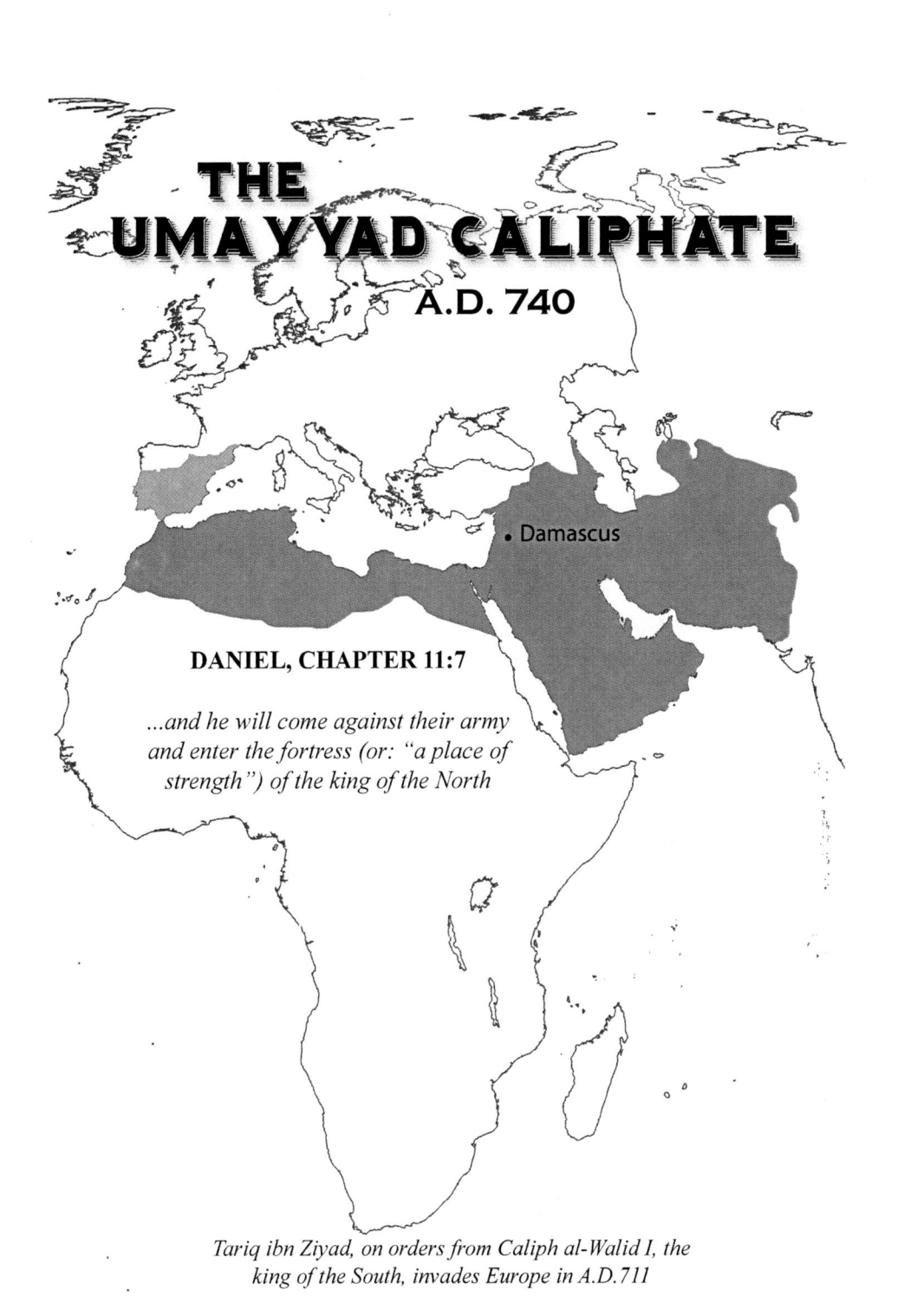

THE UMAYYAD CALIPHATE
A.D. 740

• Damascus

DANIEL, CHAPTER 11:7

...and he will come against their army and enter the fortress (or: "a place of strength") of the king of the North

Tariq ibn Ziyad, on orders from Caliph al-Walid I, the king of the South, invades Europe in A.D.711

*7. But out of a branch of her roots [Cleopatra] shall [one] rise up in his estate...
(KJV)*
Even though over 700 years have transpired in one verse (although certainly Daniel was unaware of this fact), the prophecy continues the link from Cleopatra to someone who shares a common ancestry with her. Cleopatra VII was of Hellenistic stock through Ptolemy but also of <u>Berber</u> stock through her maternal roots.[20] We are not told in the prophecy whether the angel that was speaking with Daniel specifically told him that there was such a connection or whether Daniel deduced the relation from some physical trait, such as skin color, but the point is extraneous. Historical facts confirm what prophecy states, which is that there was an ancestral connection between Cleopatra and the next major character in our unfolding human drama. By the early 700's, the Umayyad Caliphate had expanded across North Africa to what is now, Algeria. A <u>Berber</u>, Muslim, and deputy of the region, named Tariq ibn Ziyad *"rose up in his estate"* and was promoted to the rank of General by the Umayyad Caliph, Al-Walid I.

7... and he will come against their army and enter the fortress (or: "a place of strength") of the king of the North, and he will deal with them and display great strength.
In the year 711 under orders from the Caliphate, Tariq ibn Ziyad crossed over the Straits of Gibraltar *(in Arabic: gibr = rock; tar = shortened form of Tariq: i.e. "Gibr-al-tar" means "the rock of Tariq")* and invaded the Iberian Peninsula (Spain and Portugal), a place of strength of the Northern Kingdom.

Displaying *"great strength,"* he advanced for an incredible 21 years and conquered all of Spain and Southern France. The Muslim invaders were stopped in 732 near Tours, France, by Charles 'The Hammer' Martel, King of the Francs, founder of the Carolingian Empire, and grandfather of Emperor Charlemagne. Historians agree that this battle was a pivotal point in Western civilization. Had Martel failed, all of Christian Europe would have been overrun by the conquering sword of Islam.

8. And also their gods with their metal images and their precious vessels of silver and gold he will take into captivity to Egypt...
Not only in Spain, but also in Italy during the 7th through 9th centuries, Muslim invaders from Egypt plundered the gold and silver of the Roman Catholic Church. In 846 they even captured Vatican City and seized St. Peter's Basilica itself taking *images* of the Christian *gods* (saints and crucifixes) and the *precious vessels* of the Eucharist.[21]

8... and he on his part will refrain from attacking (lit. "take a stand against..." or "hold his ground against...") the king of the North for some years (lit. "a division of time").

---

[20] Christopher J. Bennett of Tyndale House, University of Cambridge, writes: "The Ptolemies... probably have the largest set of foreign dynastic connections of any ruling family in Egyptian history...the most varied set [including] Iranian, Berber, Egyptian, and Roman." http://www.geocities.com/christopherjbennett/ptolemies/affilates/aff_ptolemies.htm

[21] http://www.absoluteastronomy.com/topics/Sack_of_Rome_(846)

"...he on his part...", that is Tariq ibn Ziyad, who was able to maintain a foothold in France for literally *"a division of time"*—that is, one century. For it would take the rise of Charlemagne, Emperor of the Francs to finally push out the armies of Islam.

{ Historical Timeline—the Muslim Empire underwent a change in leadership. The Umayyad Caliphate had descended into decadence and apostasy. In 750 AD a new tribe overthrew the Umayyad Caliphate and established the Abbasid Caliphate. All of the Umayyad leaders were killed except for one man, who escaped to Spain. The city of Baghdad was built and replaced Damascus as the capital city of Islam. }

9. Then the latter (i.e. the king of the north) will enter the realm of the king of the South, but will return to his own land.[22]

By the late 8th century, Spain, Portugal, and Southern France were inarguably within the legitimate *"realm"* (also trans. *"dominion"*) of *Dar al Islam*. The Moors had immigrated into and settled the land for more than a generation—almost 70 years. Then, starting in 778, Charlemagne, in an act of war, *"entered the realm"* of the Muslim Caliphate in Europe. His armies effectively removed all Muslim forces from France by the year 811—exactly one century later as prophesied, *"a division of time."* However it would take Christian Europe seven more centuries to completely secure the Iberian Peninsula from the Muslim settlers. During his reign, Charlemagne also reconquered most of Italy from the Muslim Saracens of North Africa. Finally, in fulfillment of prophecy, Charlemagne *"returned to his own land"* to rule from France, never extending his invasion into Africa or the Middle East.

DANIEL, CHAPTER 11:7-9

7. But out of a branch of her roots shall [one] rise up in his estate and he will come against their army and enter the fortress of the king of the North, and he will deal with them and display great strength and he on his part will refrain from attacking the king of the North for some years. 9. Then the latter (i.e. the king of the north) will enter the realm of the king of the South, but will return to his own land.

Franc at Tours: In 732 AD the Francs, led by their king Charles 'The Hammer' Martel, the king of the North, ransacked the Arab camp at Tours, France effectively stopped the invading Muslim force.

---

[22] Note: translations agree 10-to-3 inferring that it is the northern king that is active here in invasion.

Godfrey of Boullion (1060-1100) storms the battlements of Jerusalem during the 1st Crusades. He would later rule as the King of Jerusalem.

{ Historical Timeline—the Muslim Seljuk Turks (a quasi-independent, military arm of the Abbasid Caliphate) had been successful in their military campaigns against the Eastern Orthodox, Byzantine Empire. Byzantium suffered a ruinous defeat to the Muslims in the *Battle of Manzikert* in 1071 which resulted in the loss of almost all of Asia Minor for the Eastern Christian Empire. }

10. And his sons will mobilize and assemble (or "stir themselves up for strife") a multitude of great forces;
In 1095, Alexios I Komemnos, Emperor of the Eastern Byzantine Kingdom sent ambassadors to Pope Urban II to request military aid against the Muslims. The resulting Council of Clermont was attended in such numbers by both cleric and laity that it was held outside the city. Daniel said they would *"stir themselves up for war..."*—and they did indeed!

Pope Urban II's sermon proved to be the single most effective speech in European history. Invoking Christ's name, Urban commanded all Christians, noble and common, rich and poor, to free the Holy Land from *"that vile race."*[23] With a promise from the Pope of forgiveness of sins as well as all monetary debts, eventually a mob numbering over 100,000 (including women and children) migrated toward the Holy Land to defeat the Turks in what history would call The First Crusade. Most would die of starvation, exposure, and disease before ever reaching Asia Minor to fight the Turks who finished off almost all that remained. Only about 1,500 knights out of 7,000 who started the journey lived to see the capture of Jerusalem in 1099. These became the founders of the renowned *Knights Templar.*

DANIEL, CHAPTER 11:10a

10. And his sons will mobilize and assemble a multitude of great forces;

Charlemagne the Great, Emporer of the Francs and king of the North, pushed the invading armies of Islam out of France in the year 811.

Catholic clergy were instrumental in rallying warriors to fight the Crusades, proclaiming, "God wills it!"

---

[23] http://www.fordham.edu/halsall/source/urban2-5vers.html

Saladin, Sultan of Egypt and Syria, was the leader of the Islamic forces during the 3rd Crusade.

Daniel stated that *"his [Charlemagne's] sons* (plural—i.e. his descendants)... *would assemble a multitude* (plural) *of great forces* (again, plural)... " The Nobility of Europe comprised mostly of French heritage would assemble multitudes of forces for the next two-hundred years to free the Holy Land from the Muslims. Here is a short, historical listing:
• 1st Crusade—1095—Raymond IV, Eustace & Baldwin Godfrey of Boulogne, Count Robert II, and others succeed in taking Jerusalem.
• 2nd Crusade—1145—Louis VII of France & Conrad III of Germany march into Jerusalem in 1147 but fail to gain any great military victories. They return to Europe in 1150.
• 1167—Sultan Shawar of Cairo of the Fatimid (Shi'ite Muslim) Dynasty calls on King Amalric I of Jerusalem, a Christian, to help defend his city against Nur Ad-din of Damascus—a Sunni Muslim.
  • Christians are massacred in Antioch; Reynard de Chatillon is captured.
  • Amalric's army is defeated outside the walls of Cairo by Saladin, who then conquers the Fatimid Dynasty of Cairo. Saladin is made Sultan of Egypt and Syria in 1171 forming the Ayyubid Dynasty.
  • Baldwin IV, the leper king, is made King of Jerusalem at age 13 in 1174. He forges a peace agreement with Saladin.
  • Reynard is released from prison and began raids—even upon Mecca.
  • Baldwin IV dies of leprosy in 1185. Baldwin V (age 5) holds the kingship of Jerusalem for one year and dies.
  • Sybille (mother of Baldwin V) crowns herself Queen and her new husband Guy de Lusignan as king in 1186.

DANIEL, CHAPTER 11:10

10. And his sons will mobilize and assemble a multitude of great forces;

Crusader knights from the 1st Crusade fight saracens at Antioch in 1096 AD.

Louis VII, King of France, is defended by his bodyguards from the surrounding Turk forces in the 2nd Crusade.

STORMING OF ACRE BY
THE CRUSADERS.

Richard the Lionheart storms the walls of Acre with an invading force during the 3rd Crusade.

- Saladin takes Tiberius in 1187. Guy is taken prisoner and eventually ransomed. Reynard is beheaded by Saladin.
• 3rd Crusade—1189-92—Richard I of England inherits the crown from his father Henry II.
  - Several battles occur between Richard "the lion-hearted" and Saladin. Richard recaptures Acre, Jaffa, and Jerusalem.
  - 1192—Richard and Saladin sign a peace treaty regarding Jerusalem. Richard and Saladin return to their homes and die in ~ 1199.
• 4th Crusade—1202-04—The Latin Crusaders, tired of fighting Muslims, instead sack Constantinople and kill all of their Orthodox brothers inside its walls.
• 1217—Al-Mu'azzam, nephew of Saladin, destroys the walls of Jerusalem to prevent its defense by future crusaders.
• 5th Crusade—1217-1221—an attempt led by John of Brienne (France) to take Jerusalem via Egypt. His forces sail to Egypt, briefly take Damietta, and besiege Cairo.
  - Saint Francis of Assisi attempts negotiation between Crusader forces and Muslim defenders—no success.
  - John fails to take Cairo and surrenders to Al-Kamil of the Ayyubids.
• 6th Crusade—1228—Holy Roman Emperor Fredrick II negotiates with an Ayyubid faction in Egypt, Al-Kamil—who had defeated the previous crusade. A 10-year truce is signed in exchange for 3 cities and Jerusalem. In 1244 the treaty expires and a rival Islamic group, the Mamelukes of Turkey, take the city of Jerusalem.

10... and one of them will keep coming and overflow and pass through, that he may again wage war up to his very fortress.

DANIEL, CHAPTER 11:10

10... and one of them will keep coming and overflow and pass through, that he may again wage war up to his very fortress.

Richard I, the Lionheart and Saladin meet at the Battle of Arsuf in 1191.

During the 4th Crusade, the Latin Crusaders sack Constantinople, setting fire to the city and killing everyone they encountered.

THE MAMELUKE SULTINATE
A.D. 1246

DANIEL, CHAPTER 11:11

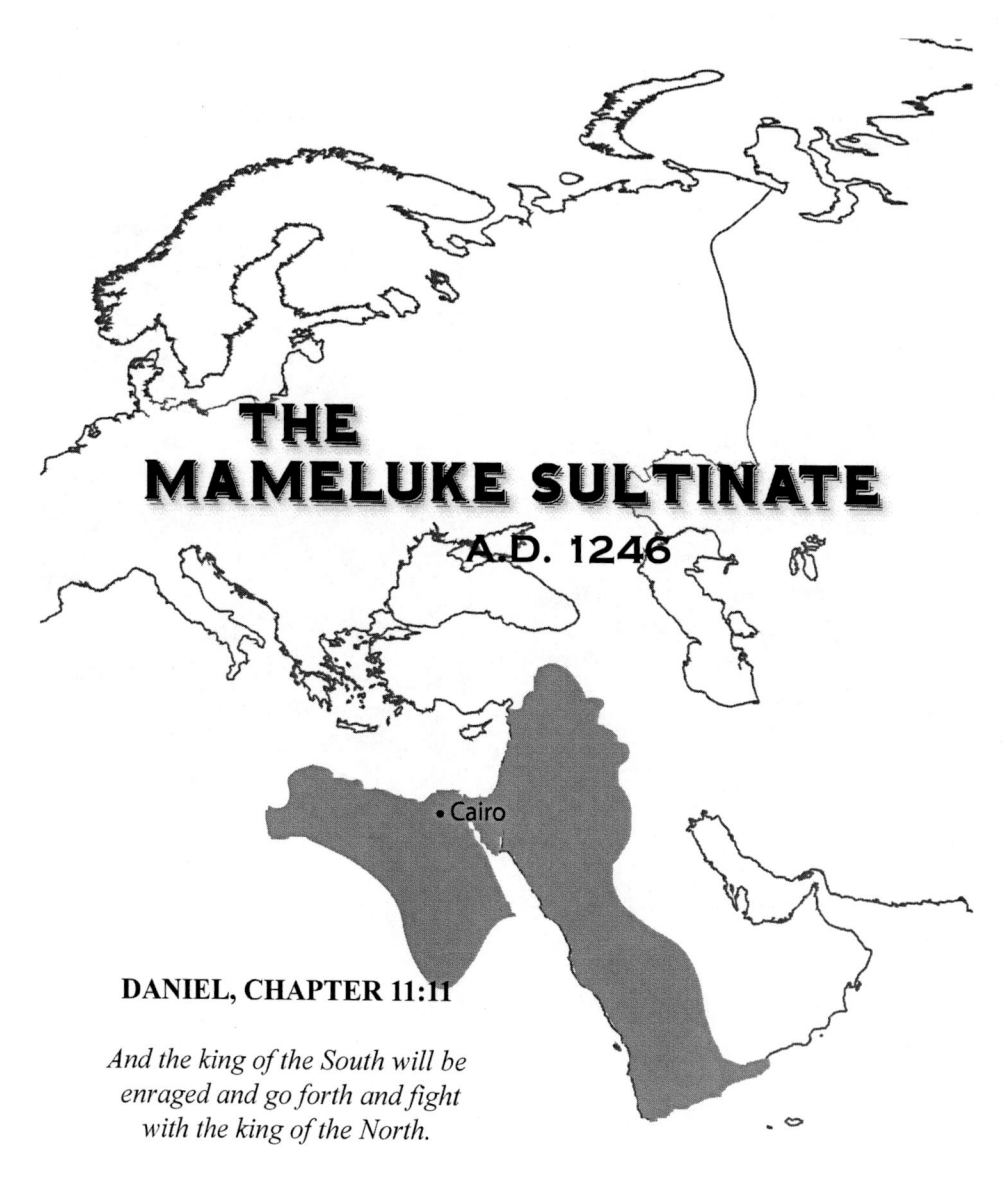

And the king of the South will be enraged and go forth and fight with the king of the North.

Sultan Baibars, the king of the South

Crusader soldiers of the 5th Crusade arrive at the Egyptian port of Damietta in 1219.

With great efficiency of words, Daniel relates two attempts by the sons of the king of the north to take *"his very* fortress," that is Cairo, Egypt, the capital of the Ayyubids—from the king of the south. The first attempt occurred during the 5th Crusade by John of Brienne. This second attempt is made in person by Emperor Louis IX of France:
- 7th Crusade—1249—Emperor Louis IX (France) lands in Egypt, takes Damietta, Egypt, and besieges the Ayyubids in Cairo.
    - o   The Mamelukes again, led by a Turkish General named Baibars, arrive from the north and defeat Louis IX outside the walls of Cairo.
    - o   Louis is captured and ransomed.
    - o   The Mamelukes then defeat the Ayyubids and take Cairo, controlling Islam from Syria to Egypt and across North Africa.

11. And the king of the South will be enraged and go forth and fight with the king of the North.
The Mamelukes led by Baibars attack the Crusader fortress cities, capturing them one-by-one. Tens of thousands of Christians are slaughtered and enslaved. By 1268 only the strongholds of Tripoli, Lebanon, and the fortress at Acre remain in the Crusaders' hands.

{ Historical Timeline—The Crusades were pivotal events in the history of Europe, but for *Dar al Islam* being spread across two continents, it was but a minor flesh wound. The mortal attack however, as prophesied by Jeremiah[24], would come from

---
[24] In my book The *Chronicles of Babylon* I go into these prophecies of Jeremiah in great detail—db.

Islam's northeastern border by the hordes of Genghis Khan. In the late 12th century with the inevitability of an approaching hurricane, Genghis Khan hammered the armies of Islam, taking the regions of Uzbekistan and Afghanistan. In the winter of 1258 under the command of Hülagü Khan, grandson of Genghis Khan, the great city of Baghdad was besieged. Within two weeks' time the city fell. As one historian put it, "[The Mongols] swept through the city like hungry falcons attacking a flight of doves."[25] All 900,000 of the city's inhabitants were put to the sword. The treasury was raided, and the very culture of Islam was destroyed with the city. This Mongol destruction of Baghdad inflicted a spiritual and psychological mortal wound from which Islam has yet to recover. }

- 8th Crusade—1270—Emperor Louis IX dies of dysentery while besieging Tunis in North Africa. The siege is abandoned due to further illness. The Sultan of Tunis grants access to Tunis to Christian traders and monks.

11…Then the latter [the king of the North] will raise a great multitude, but that multitude will be given into the hand of the former.
The 9th Crusade—1271— is in retaliation to the continued growth and power of the Mameluk Empire (centered in Cairo, Egypt) under Sultan Baibars. Prince Edward I of England ("Longshanks"—of *Braveheart* fame) is too late to help Louis IX in Tunis and so continues to Tripoli, Lebanon, to assist

---

[25] Abdullah Wassaf as cited by historian Dr. David Morgan, professor of History at University of Wisconsin—Madison in his book, *The Mongols*, Blackwell Publishing, 2007, ISBN 1405135395

DANIEL, CHAPTER 11:11-12

11. And the king of the South will be enraged and go forth and fight with the king of the North. Then the latter [the king of the North] will raise a great multitude, but that multitude will be given into the hand of the former. 12. When the multitude is carried away, his heart will be lifted up, and he will cause tens of thousands to fall; yet he will not prevail..

The Mamelukes, led by Sultan Baibars, the king of the South, drove the crusaders out of their fortress cities one-by-one.

Edward I of England (Longshanks) and his army fought in futility against the strong forces of the Mamelukes.

in the battle against the Mamelukes. Edward's attempts at Tripoli and later in an attack on the city of Qaqun were futile. The Mamelukes were distracted from totally annihilating the Crusaders because of a coordinated attack on their northern border by the Mongol forces of Abaqa Khan, son of Hülagü Khan. Under the leadership of General Samagar, the Mongols devastated the region of Alepo, Syria, but made a hasty retreat back across the Euphrates on news of Baibars' massive counter offensive. Prince Edward barely survives an assassination attempt and a few months later is informed of the death of his father, King Henry III. Due to the steadily deteriorating situation for the Christian forces, a hasty truce is signed with Baibars thus allowing Edward to leave to assume the throne of England.

12. When the multitude is carried away, his heart will be lifted up, and he will cause tens of thousands to fall; yet he will not prevail.
In 1291, Sultan Qalawun (Baibars's successor) attacks the last, remaining Crusader fortress at Acre with many losses. Qalawun himself does *"not prevail"* but dies before taking the city. His son, General Khalil, becomes Sultan and captures Acre. Khalil, in retaliation for perceived treacheries, multiple treaty violations and a botched surrender by the Crusaders, executes the majority of the inhabitants, soldier and civilian alike, and enslaves the remainder—exactly as prophesied.

{ Historical Timeline—after almost 200 years the Crusades are completed with neither side gaining any significant territory. In 1453 the Byzantine city of Constantinople finally fell to the Ottoman Turks who renamed the city "Istanbul". The Black Plague which devastated Europe and the Mediterranean during the middle 1300's retarded the rapid expansion of the Ottoman Empire northward, as did continuous attacks on their eastern frontier by the Mongols. Also, in the mid-to-late 1400's Vlad III Dracula of Wallachia proved to be a pain in the neck to Sultan Mehmed II and prevented further expansion northward. In the year 1492 under the Monarchy of Ferdinand of Spain, the Muslims are finally pushed out of the Iberian Peninsula.}

13. For the king of the North will again raise a greater multitude than the former, and after an interval of some years he will press on with a great army and much equipment.
In 1798 Napoleon Bonaparte, the new *"king of the North"*, invaded Egypt with an army of 35,000 men, heavy cavalry, and cannons (*"much equipment"*), conquering Cairo and both Lower and Upper Egypt. He defeated the Mamelukes in battle-after-battle. The passage *"...after an interval of some years..."* may also be translated *"at the end of an epoch (fixed unit of time)"*. This is true on a couple of levels:
    1) It occurred at the end of half-a-millennium (from 1291 to 1798 is at the end of 500 years)
    2) It occurred at the end of the Renaissance, an identifiable time period in European history.

Napoleon Bonaparte invaded Egypt with an army of 35,000 men, heavy cavalry and cannons "...with a great army and much equipment."

{ Historical Timeline—Napoleon conquered most of Syria but did not take Acre. The political center-of-gravity of *"the South"* had already shifted north to Istanbul and the Turks of the Ottoman Empire. The loss of the two metropolitan cities of Cairo and Damascus to Napoleon initiated the erosion of the Ottoman Empire as we see next. In the north, major events are also soon to occur. Napoleon is defeated at the Battle of Waterloo in 1815 and the new capital for the king of the North shifts from Paris to Moscow, home of the Czars of the Russian Empire. }

14. Now in those times many will rise up against the king of the South;
During *"those times"* of the 1800's the rise of nationalism began to rip apart the Ottoman Empire piece by piece.
• 1829—Greece declared independence from the Ottoman Turks
• Proto-Zionism—early 1800
  • Elijah ben Soloman of Lithuania, known as the Vilna Gaon, was one of the most influential rabbinic

DANIEL, CHAPTER 11:13

13. For the king of the North will again raise a greater multitude than the former, and after an interval of some years he will press on with a great army and much equipment.

Napoléon Bonaparte (1769–1821), first Emperor of France and the "king of the North" in 1798.

DISMANTLING OF THE OTTOMAN EMPIRE
1798-1923

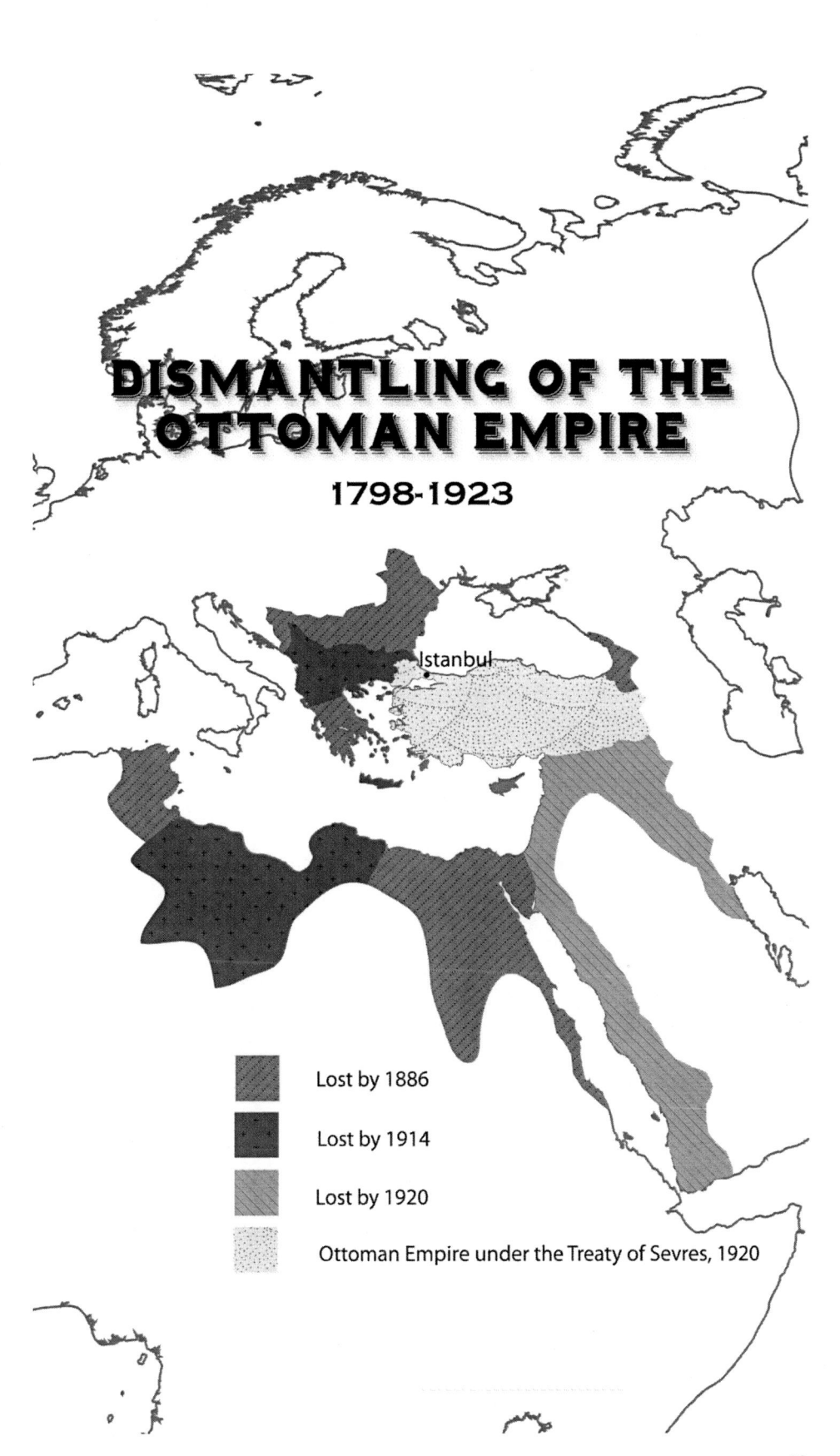

Istanbul

- Lost by 1886
- Lost by 1914
- Lost by 1920
- Ottoman Empire under the Treaty of Sevres, 1920

authorities since the Middle Ages. He influenced over 500 of his followers to make *aliyah*[26] to Palestine in the years from 1808-1812.[27]
- 1836—Rabbi Kalischer petitioned Baron Rothschild of the United Kingdom to buy Palestine or at least the Temple Mount from the Turks.
- 1839—Sir Moses Montefiore, also of the U.K., attempted negotiations with the Turks for the land of Palestine.[28]
- 1840's—A Serbian Jew, Rabbi Yehuda Solomon Alkali wrote articles stating that Jews must return to Palestine to hasten the coming of Messiah and as a precondition for the redemption of the Jewish people. He encouraged a return to Zion and independence for Israel during this time.[29]
- 1875—Serbia, Montenegro, Bosnia, Wallachia, and Moldova declared independence from the Ottoman Empire.
- 1877-78—the Russo-Turkish War granted independence to Serbia, Romania, Montenegro, and Bulgaria
- 1912—the Ottomans lost Libya to Italy during the Italo-Turkish War

14...the violent ones (also "robbers", or "sons of breakage") among your people will also lift themselves up in order to fulfill the vision...
These *"robbers"* attempted to *"fulfill the vision"* of the Rabbis Alkali and Kalischer—that is, the emancipation of the Jews. For many, this meant a return to Israel and the formation of a Jewish State. Though some of these groups were religious in nature, the main Zionist / emancipation movements at this time in history came from atheist Jewry who will *"lift themselves up in order to fulfill the vision..."* (emphasis added). Some of the atheists of Jewish heritage of the mid-1800's, who lifted up themselves were:
- Karl Marx, a Prussian Jew who coauthored the *Communist Manifesto* and is the indisputable father of Marxist-socialism. *"My object in life is to dethrone God and destroy capitalism."*[30] In Marx's booklet, *On the Jewish Question* (1844), he writes, *"We must emancipate ourselves before we emancipate others."*[31] The booklet is a condemnation of all religions as well as all private property ownership. Quoting from the same source again, Marx writes, *"the existence of religion is the existence of defect"* and he encourages the destruction of both religion and private property *"to the maximum."* That is, by the guillotine if necessary. In his closing remarks, he makes this incredibly chilling statement, *"In the final analysis, the emancipation of the Jews is the emancipation of mankind from Judaism."*[32]
- Moses Hess, a German Jew, turned first to utopian and then to scientific socialism. An atheist, Hess was credited for several "Marxian" slogans including, *"Religion is the opiate of the masses."* He was a friend and collaborator of Karl Marx and converted Friedrich Engels to Communism, who later joined Marx as coauthor of the *Communist Manifesto.*
- Leon Trotsky—Ukrainian Jew and Bolshevik revolutionary, second only to Vladimir Lenin. As head of the Red Army, he was responsible for the deaths of mil-

---

[26] The term *aliyah* refers to the immigration of Jews to the land of Israel. In Hebrew it means ascent.
[27] http://www.absoluteastronomy.com/topics/Vilna_Gaon
[28] http://www.chabad.org/library/article_cdo/aid/112353/jewish/Sir-Moses-Montefiore.htm
[29] http://www.zionism-israel.com/brief_zionism_history.htm
[30] http://quotes.liberty-tree.ca/quote/karl_marx_quote_ebab
[31] *On the Jewish Question*, translated by Blunden, Grant and Carmody, 2008/9.

lions in the Russian Civil War against anti-communist Russians and their allies.[33]

Regarding the terms *"...the violent ones, robbers, or sons of breakage"*, all three terms aptly describe these atheistic communists of Jewish ancestry. For the sons *"break"* from the traditions of a hundred generations of Jews before them, denying the very existence of the God of the Hebrews. And they are *"robbers"*, for at its heart, disguised in a veil of so-called "equity", Communism/Socialism exists by stealing from the "haves" to give to the "have not's"—robbery that was legalized by Bolshevik fiat, but "robbery" nonetheless. And communists and socialists by whatever name, are unquestionably the most *"violent"* people on earth, all the while preaching peace.

Communism has been tried in numerous places on this globe; the USSR, China, Viet Nam, Cambodia, Korea, and Cuba to name a few; and always with the same outcome—tens of millions exterminated, billions enslaved, rampant poverty, and a bankrupt economy. This ideology of *"redistribution of wealth"*[34] along with companion terms like, *"political and economic justice,"*[35] is an insidious and malevolent theory conceived in Hell itself and disguised in a cloak of altruism and counterfeit compassion. Its true objective, however, has never changed—the domination and enslavement of the individual to the will of the State.

14...but they will fall down.
• 1st Aliyah (1870's) ~25,000 socialist-Zionists immigrated to Palestine and set up Kibbutz based upon the writings of

DANIEL, CHAPTER 11:14

14. Now in those times many will rise up against the king of the South; the violent ones (also "robbers", or "sons of breakage") among your people will also lift themselves up in order to fulfill the vision but they will fall down.

Karl Marx, a Jew from Prussia, wrote the Communist manifesto in 1848.
"...the violent ones among your people."

---

[32] *ibid*
[33] Casualties: Red Army--over 1.2 million; White Army—at least 1 million; civilians—over 13 million. http://en.wikipedia.org/wiki/Russian_Civil_War
[34] Sen. Barack Obama, 2001, Chicago Public Radio-WBEZ.FM
[35] *ibid*

Marx and Hess but most returned home defeated by disease, poverty and unemployment.
- 2nd Aliyah (1909) ~85,000 socialist-Zionists immigrated to Palestine. These were scorned by the indigenous Arab populations for lack of stamina, language, and salary needs. They also failed to settle permanently in Palestine.

{ <u>Historical Timeline:</u> At this time (1875 to 1880) and subsequent to Napoleon's defeat at Waterloo, the Russian Empire had the largest standing army in the world and covered the largest land mass, extending even into present day Alaska. Due to the Balkan Crisis (the previously mentioned declarations of independence from the Ottomans by the Balkan states in 1875), Russian armies invaded and captured a great deal of Ottoman territory. }

15. Then the king of the North will come, cast up a siege mound, and capture a well-fortified city; and the forces of the South will not stand their ground, not even their choicest troops, for there will be no strength to make a stand.
After the defeat of Emperor Napoleon at the Battle of Waterloo in 1815, Czar Alexander II of the Russian Empire emerged as the new *"king of the North"*. Alexander's adversary was Sultan Abdul Hammed II, *"the king of the South"* of the Ottoman Empire. Sultan Hammed was also known by his European subjects by more colorful terms like "Hammed the butcher" or "Hammed the damned." The Muslims had held the Eastern Orthodox Balkan States of Bulgaria, Romania, Bosnia, etc. for approximately 500 years. With the rise of nationalism in these Balkan States, Russia saw an opportunity not only to regain some territory that was lost in the Crimean War but also to liberate the Orthodox Christians from cruel Muslim oppression and extend Russia's spiritual and political influence. The decisive battle in the Russo-Turkish War (1877-1878) was the siege of the *"well fortified"* city of Pleven, Bulgaria.

The Russian Army besieged the city of Pleven and, with the aid of a Romanian contingent, took the city after a 5 month siege, capturing the Turkish Field Marshal, Osman Pasha, along with *"his choicest troops."* The defense of the siege of Pleven was lauded on both sides of the conflict by Czar and generals alike. Russia forced the Ottoman surrender and, under the Treaty of San Stefano, divested the Ottomans of all their holdings in Europe with the exception of the area immediately surrounding Istanbul.

16. But he who comes against him will do as he pleases and no one will be able to withstand him;
Here Daniel makes an abrupt change of direction. He had been speaking in the previous verse about the king of the North and the inability of the king of the South to withstand him, *"not even his choicest troops"*. But then, someone comes against the king of the North *"and no one will be able to withstand him;"* Given the previous statement about his *"choicest troops"* it would be illogical to conclude that Daniel intended for this to mean the king of the South. And consistent with the previous verses throughout the chapter he would have made a more direct reference such as: the former, the latter, or even the king of the South. The very lack of such a qualifying statement shows us that Daniel is indeed referring to a third-party who has now entered the fray and by inference, since he is coming against the king of the North, he too is from the North.

This is the first reference in Chapter Eleven regarding civil-war (if it can be called that) within the Empire of the North. The *"he"* who came against Czar Alexander II of the Russian Empire (i.e. the king of the North) was Kaiser Wilhelm I, King of Prussia and 1st German Emperor. So how was this portion of verse 16 fulfilled in history?

Alarmed at the Russian Expansion, the Germans, British, and French forced the Russians to attend the Congress of Berlin hosted by Prussian President/German Chancellor Otto von Bismarck. Due to the Congress of Berlin, Russia was forced to relinquish 18 of the 29 articles of surrender gained at the Treaty of San Stefano. Kaiser Wilhelm I succeeded where others had failed for a thousand years. By pulling together various Germanic kings and rulers (like Baden and Bavaria) he created a unified Germany, making it one of the most powerful European countries at the time. And, speaking in the future aspect again, Daniel states that *"no one will be able to withstand"* this German Emperor.

16... he will also stay for a time in the Beautiful (or desirable or glorious) Land...
The capitalization of the term *"Beautiful Land"* in the NASV is a commentary, not a translation, since Hebrew has no capital letters. The translators of certain versions (NKJV, NIV, and NLB) wished to infer (or in some cases actually name) that the land of Israel was intended here but this a mere holdover from the traditional interpretation of this chapter. The literal meaning is simply: *"glorious land... desirable land... land of beauty".*[36]

---

[36] Hebrew Names Version, Young's Literal Translation, Darby Translation, and Noah Webster Translation.

DANIEL, CHAPTER 11:15-16

15. Then the king of the North will come, cast up a siege mound, and capture a well-fortified city; and the forces of the South will not stand their ground, not even their choicest troops, for there will be no strength to make a stand. 16. But he who comes against him will do as he pleases and no one will be able to withstand him; he will also stay for a time in the Beautiful (or desirable or glorious) Land...

Czar Alexander II, king of the North in 1816
"...the king of the North will come...and capture a well-fortified city"

Sultan Abdul Hammed II
"...the forces of the South will not stand their ground."

47

Kaiser Wilhelm I was the King of Prussia (1861 to 1888) and the first German Emperor from 1871 to 1888. In 1878 the Kaiser came against the king of the north, "...but no one will be able to withstand him."

The beautiful and much desired land here was the Alsace-Lorraine region of France that the German Empire was soon to acquire. During the time of Bismarck, Kaiser Wilhelm I instigated the Franco-Prussian War (1870). France was routed in every battle. Germany acquired the Alsace-Lorraine area, and Wilhelm was crowned Emperor of Germany in the Palace of Versailles, which was situated within the Alsace-Lorraine region. This region encompasses the Rhine and Moselle River valleys and is known not only for the excellent vineyards but also for the great Rhine River, which serves as a border as well as providing a vital, navigable waterway. The existence of a multitude of castles and fortifications along the Rhine bear witness to its strategic and monetary importance to both France and Germany.

DANIEL, CHAPTER 11:16-17

16...by which his hand (i.e. strength) shall be consumed... (NWV)

After winning the war, Chancellor Otto von Bismarck strongly opposed attaining this territory that he knew would provoke the French into a sustained enmity with the German Empire. However, Kaiser Wilhelm felt that the strategic, military and economic advantage was worth the troubles it would cause. It was the acquisition of this land that caused such retribution by the French after W.W.I and consumed his strength.

17. And he will set his face to come with the power of his whole kingdom, bringing with him a proposal of peace which he will put into effect...

Kaiser Wilhelm I signed the Three Emperors League with Russia and Austria-Hungary in 1872, and later in 1887 after the previous alliance broke down, he signed the Reinsurance Treaty in an attempt to continue his alliance with Russia. This was an alliance not just with the Kingdom of Prussia, but with the entire German Empire, hence: *"the power of his whole kingdom."* His successor, Wilhelm II later signed a secret non-aggression agreement with Czar Nicholas II (his cousin-in-law) in 1905.

17... and he shall give him the daughter of women...

Princess Alix of Hess was the daughter of Duke Louis IV of Hess, Germany. She was German on her father's side and English on her mother's side making her the granddaughter of Queen Victoria of Great Britain. This made her 1st cousin to Emperor Wilhelm II who was also a grandchild of Queen Victoria. Princes Alix's marriage to Czar Nicholas II in 1894 made the Kaiser and the Czar cousins-in-law. The two rulers were genuinely close to one another, writing considerable letters back and forth for over

16...by which his hand shall be consumed 17. And he will set his face to come with the power of his whole kingdom, bringing with him a proposal of peace which he will put into effect and he shall give him the daughter of women, corrupting her but she will not take a stand for him or be on his side.

Nicholas II and Alexandra Fyodorovna, Czar and Czarista of Russia

Rasputin, a Russian mystic and faith-healer held considerable influence over Czar Nicholas II and Czarista Alexandra.

two decades, almost always closing the letters with, *"your affectionate cousin."*[37] They expressed a sincere concern for the other's children, especially the young Czarevich, Alexei Romanov who suffered from the fatal genetic disorder of hemophilia. With regards to the specifics of the Kaiser's personal influence mentioned in this verse, the following quote buttresses the point,

"Wilhelm II as Kaiser took a special interest in Alix. As a young man he had frequently visited her family. ...Now Kaiser Wilhelm and others strongly advised Alix to accept the marriage offer of Tsar Nicholas. Wilhelm had gotten on badly with Nicholas' father, Tsar Alexander III. He hoped to return to good graves by brokering the marriage and perhaps help move Russia away from the dangerous alliance with France."[38]

17...corrupting her (HNV)...
A German-Protestant since childhood, Alexandra converted to Russian Orthodox and became corrupted by the sorceries of Grigori Rasputin, the Russian mystic, charlatan/faith-healer. The Czarista, however, considered him to be a prophet and a holy man. Thus Rasputin became the gate keeper for anyone desiring an audience with the royal couple, despite the fact that he had been accused by many eminent persons of unrestricted sex orgies and raping a nun.

17. But she will not take a stand for him or be on his side.
After her marriage to Czar Nicholas II, she changed her name to the Russian, "Alexandra Fyodorovna," Czarista of Russia. Though she was seen in her country of Russia as a hard German, when push came to shove, she sided with Russia and the Czar—not the side of Germany or her cousin, the Kaiser. Sadly, neither Alexandra, Czar Nicholas, nor any of the royal family would live to see the end World War I. The entire Romanov family was brutally murdered by the Bolsheviks in February 1917, during the socialist revolution.

18. Then he will turn his face to (or "lay his hands violently upon") the coastlands and capture many...
Daniel is still speaking here of Emperor Wilhelm II of Germany & King of Prussia who through a series of treaties was compelled into "The Great War" in 1914, and through this war attempted to spread Pan-German nationalism by *"laying his hands violently upon the coastlands"*. The word *"coastlands"* is a bit ambiguous in Hebrew and is also translated, *"habitable land."* At its height, the War encompassed all of Europe and the Middle East—to and including India, north-south-& east Africa, Pacific islands, and every ocean and sea on the globe. Germany *"captured many"* as the scripture states. During the War, the Central Powers (Germany and her allies) held almost 4.5 million men as prisoners of war, most of these from Russia. Approximately half of the Russian POW's died in captivity. Altogether, almost 16 million military and civilians on both sides of the conflict died as a direct result of the war.[39]

---

[37] See the Willy-Nicky Papers.
[38] histclo.com/Royal/rus/n2/n2-alix.htm
[39] http://en.wikipedia.org/wiki/World_War_I_casualties

18. But a commander will put a stop to his scorn against him; moreover, he will repay him for his scorn.

By 1916 after two grueling years of war, the Kaiser was mentally overcome by the war effort and had become only a figurehead. The empire had come to be ruled by Field Marshal Paul von Hindenburg and his 2nd in command, General Wilhelm Groener (in 1918). In 1918 during the War, the German Revolt took place. Weary from the war and the scorn exhibited by the rest of the world toward Germany, 40,000 German sailors revolted and refused to continue the fight. The Kaiser initially attempted to have the first instigators tried and hung for desertion, but the rank-and-file servicemen (and by this time the Generals) would not allow his *"scorn"* of the military to proceed. General Groener (repaying the scorn) informed Kaiser Wilhelm II that he must step down from the throne and that his (Groener's) army would not fight to preserve the monarchy. Field Marshal Hindenburg was also obliged to advise Wilhelm to abdicate the throne. In the ensuing anarchy, both communists and monarchists attempted to take over the country.

19. So he will turn his face toward the fortresses of his own land, but he will stumble and fall and be found no more.

When it became evident that defeat of Germany in the War was inevitable, Wilhelm *"turned his face toward the fortress of his own land"* of Prussia with the intent of preserving the monarchy by force. Even if forced to give up the German Empire, he hoped to remain King of Prussia. However, he *"stumbled and fell"* when the Chancellor, Prince Max of Baden, unexpectedly announced Wilhelm's abdication of the kingship of Prussia and offered an unconditional surrender and cease-fire to U.S. Presi-

DANIEL, CHAPTER 11:18-19

18. Then he will turn his face to (or "lay his hands violently upon") the coastlands and capture many...But a commander will put a stop to his scorn against him; moreover, he will repay him for his scorn. 19. So he will turn his face toward the fortresses of his own land, but he will stumble and fall and be found no more.

General Wilhelm Groener "...put a stop to his scorn against him."

Gustav Stresemann was Chancellor of Germany during the 6-year "Golden Age" of the Weimar Republic. He was "...a raiser of taxes."

dent, Woodrow Wilson. Wilhelm II, the once King of Prussia and Emperor of all of Germany, crossed the border the next day into the Kingdom of the Netherlands where he had been assured protection and political asylum by Queen Wilhelmina. Wilhelm took with him two rail cars of royal treasures that allowed him to purchase the estate of *Huis Doorn* where he lived in exile and obscurity for the remaining 21 years of his life—and thus he was *"found no more."*

{ Historical Timeline—When Germany was unable to pay war reparations to France and Belgium, France invaded and took over the industrial Ruhr region of Germany. The German workers in response went on strike. In order to repay the debt, the German government started printing Papiermark with abandonment. The currency devalued from 4.2 per US dollar in 1914 to 4.2 trillion per US dollar in 1923.}

20. Then shall stand up in his estate a raiser of taxes [in] the glory [jewel or riches] of the kingdom: but within few days he shall be destroyed (broken), neither in anger, nor in battle. (NWV)
In 1923 Gustav Stresemann, a member of the Reichstag (parliament) *"[stood] up in his estate"* and was elected Reichskanzler (Chancellor), and thus began the 6-year "Golden Age" of the Weimar Republic (Hindenburg was still President of the military). Stresemann issued a new currency equal to the previous value of 4.2 per US dollar to halt the hyperinflation, cut government spending, and *"raised taxes."* He signed the Locarno Treaties which allowed the western powers to withdraw from the Rhineland. He signed the Dawes Plan, allowing France to vacate the Ruhr industrial region—the financial *"jewel of the kingdom"* –and tied war reparations to Germany's ability to pay, aided by US loans. Germany was also admitted to the League of Nations. In 1926 Stresemann shared the Nobel Peace Prize with Aristide Briand of France. Stresemann died in office of a heart attack in 1929 at the young age of 51, and thus he was broken, yet *"neither in anger, nor in battle."*

21. And in his place a despicable person will arise, on whom the honor of kingship has not been conferred, but he will come in a time of tranquility and seize the kingdom by intrigue (or flatteries).
In 1932, the Nazi[40] party won only 33% of the vote and of seats in the Reichstag. During the election, Hitler promised the Nationalization of: *Muterschutz*—care for pregnant mothers, *Kinderschutz*—care for young children in government run Kindergarten, and *Volksgesundheit*—a National Health Care system. Hitler used propaganda, such as blaming Jews and communists for Germany's economic woes, as well as feigning humility and *"flattery"* toward the aging President Hindenburg and making hollow promises to the Catholic Party in order to seize total dictatorial powers from the German government.

After the election, President Hindenburg was reluctantly persuaded to appoint Adolf Hitler as Chancellor, or head of the Reichstag, in what proved to be a futile attempt to pacify the Nazis. Soon thereafter, the passage of the Enabling Act by the Reichstag allowed Hitler to make and pass laws totally independent of the Legislature. In 1934 his Gestapo and SS assassinated almost 100 political and opposition leaders. When

President Hindenburg died in 1934, Hitler's cabinet declared the office of the President to be dormant and transferred all military powers to Hitler, now proclaiming him as *Führer*, or "leader".

22. And the overflowing forces will be flooded away before him and shattered, and also the prince of the covenant.

Here Daniel looks back in reference to the *"overflowing forces"* of France and Great Britain that only 20 years earlier had defeated the Kaisers' mighty army and then he leap-frogs ahead to a time in the not-too-distant future (depicted in verse 24) when these forces will themselves be *"flooded away"* before Hitler's military. Two elements of this verse buttress this interpretation:

    1) The phrase *"will be flooded away"* is in the imperative aspect, predicting a future event
    2) This is the first mention of the *"Prince of the Covenant,"* and by implication a covenant or treaty that will apparently be signed.

The *"Prince of the Covenant"* was none other than the British Prime Minister, Neville Chamberlain, who in Sept. 1938 confidently proclaimed to the people of Britain, "Peace for our time…," as he waved the agreement papers before them. But he would soon find England and the French *"flooded away"* before the Nazi army and out of the European mainland within a three-month time period by the blitzkrieg of 1940.

---

[40] The term *Nazi*, is a shortened form of the National Socialist Party. The Nazi's believed in Nationalism, or governmental control, over all of the private sector.

DANIEL, CHAPTER 11:20-22

20. Then shall stand up in his estate a raiser of taxes [in] the glory [jewel or riches] of the kingdom: but within few days he shall be destroyed, neither in anger, nor in battle. 21. And in his place a despicable person will arise, on whom the honor of kingship has not been conferred, but he will come in a time of tranquility and seize the kingdom by intrigue. 22. And the overflowing forces will be flooded away before him and shattered, and also the prince of the covenant.

Adolf Hitler, the "…despicable person."

"Peace in our time…" proclaimed Prime Minister Chamberlain, "…the Prince of the Covenant."

{ Historical Timeline—What followed Hitler's initial rise to power was a *"time of tranquility,"* as the scriptures state:
• There were no hot wars in Europe or the Middle East.
• Hitler expanded the German army to 600,000 men—six times the number allowed under the Versailles Treaty. He established a *Luftwaffe* (air force) and expanded the Navy.
• In February 1936, Nazi Germany hosted the Winter Olympic Games.
• On a Saturday in March of 1936 in violation of the Versailles Treaty, Hitler sent his army into the Rhineland—they entered unopposed, riding on bicycles while the French were busy with elections and the British Parliament members were home for the weekend and couldn't do anything until Monday when it was too late.
• In August 1936, Nazi Germany hosted the Summer Olympic Games.
• In 1938, Hitler's army marched into Vienna, Austria, for "German Re-unification" and into the Sudetenland of Czechoslovakia for the same reason. At the Munich Agreement (Sept. 1938), Britain and France gave away to Germany the entire region of Czechoslovakia—whose representatives were conspicuously absent from this meeting. This is the "<u>covenant</u>" that was written about in verse 22 and signed by the *"Prince"* himself, Prime Minister Neville Chamberlain.}

23. And after an alliance is made with him he will practice deception, and he will go up and gain power with a small force of people.
On August 23, 1939, the Molotov-Ribbentrop Pact was signed between the USSR and Nazi Germany. It was ostensibly a non-aggression pact, *"an alliance,"* between Hitler and Joseph Stalin, the cruel dictator of the Soviet Union. But included in the pact was a secret protocol wherein the two agreed to divide Northern and Eastern Europe, including Poland, between them. *"Practicing deception,"* Hitler marched into Poland with little resistance.

{ Historical Timeline— By 1940 Hitler had established an Axis alignment with Spain, Italy, Japan, Hungary, Romania, and Bulgaria.}

24. In a time of tranquility he will enter the richest parts of the realm...
"In a time of tranquility..." Also translated: *"Without warning"* (NLT & ESV); *"When the richest provinces feel secure..."* (NIV). The word *"enter"* can also be translated *"to fall upon"* or *"to attack"*.
Here is my paraphrase incorporating the meanings of all translations: *"Without warning, in a time of peace, he is going to fall upon the richest parts of the realm..."*

This of course Hitler did. In three short months—from April 4, 1940 to June 25, 1940— the Third Reich conquered Norway, Sweden, Denmark, the Netherlands, Belgium, Luxemburg and France.

24 ...and he will accomplish what his fathers never did nor his ancestors; he will distribute plunder, booty, and possessions among them...
Hitler distributed the *"plunder, booty, and possessions"* of the conquered lands to his officers in the SS, Gestapo, and the military. Included in the booty were priceless works of art and jewelry. The Nazis raided homes of the wealthy and multiple art gal-

NAZI BLITZKREIG (1940)

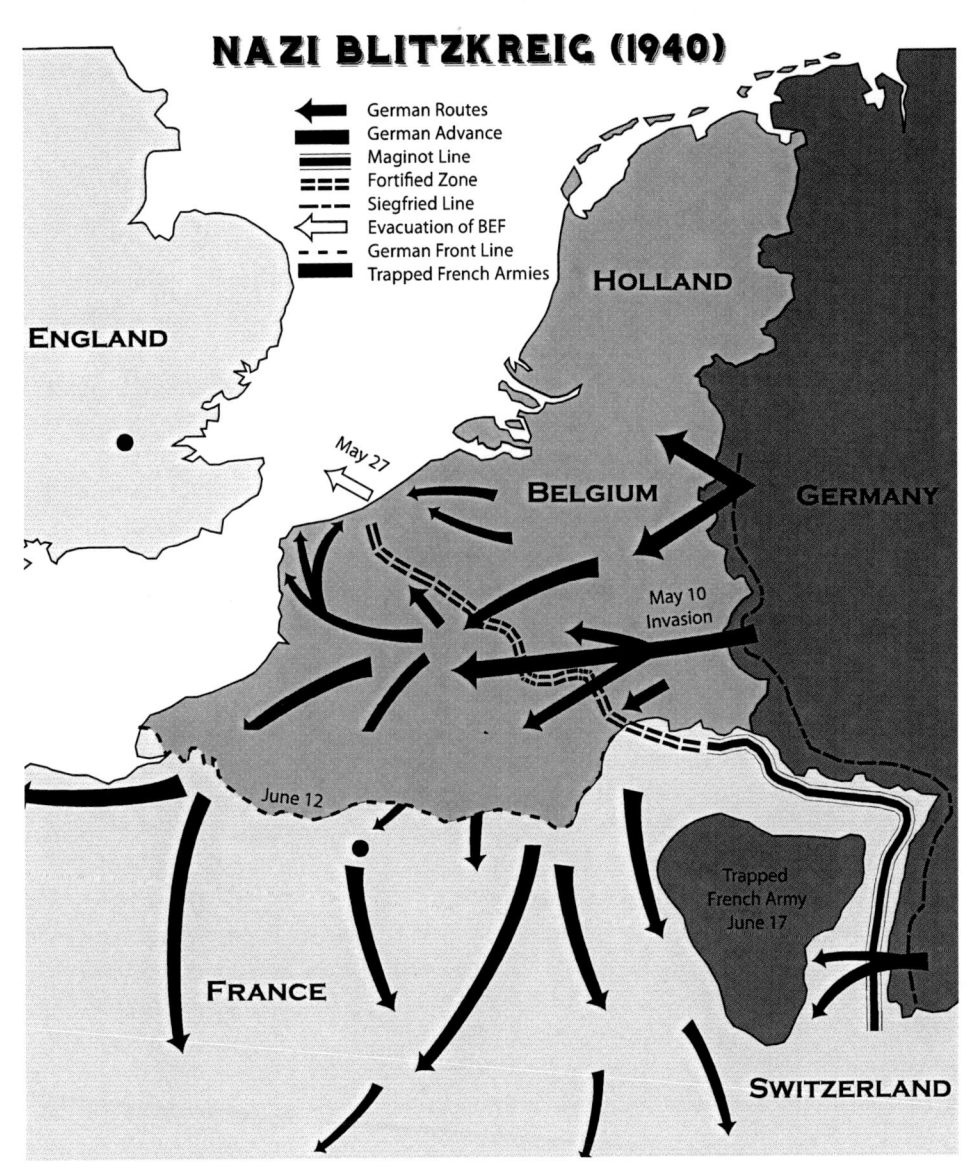

- German Routes
- German Advance
- Maginot Line
- Fortified Zone
- Siegfried Line
- Evacuation of BEF
- German Front Line
- Trapped French Armies

ENGLAND

HOLLAND

BELGIUM

GERMANY

May 27

May 10 Invasion

June 12

Trapped French Army June 17

FRANCE

SWITZERLAND

The Bleitzkreig of 1940, "...he will enter the richest parts of the realm."

leries throughout Europe including the Louvre in Paris, France. A recent book and documentary called, *The Rape of Europa[41]* chronicles the plunder and booty that Hitler distributed among the Nazi officials. These included:
- 600,000 priceless works of art (paintings, sculptures, and Jewish antiquities)
- 27 paintings by Rembrandt
- Paintings by Reuben
- Engravings by Durer
- More than 23 tons of gold was recovered from one bank vault

It is estimated that at least 100,000 pieces of art and artifacts have yet to be recovered.

24... and he will devise his schemes against strongholds, but only for a time
Hitler devised his schemes against the strongholds of Great Britain, the USSR, and the United States.

{ Historical Timeline— Looking back at the years between 1860 through the end of World War I, the nations of Europe had aggressively divided up the African continent and the Middle East. Most of Africa was held by either Britain or France (except for Libya which was held by Italy). Due to the fledgling industrial revolution and the need for petroleum products, Great Britain's greatest expansion of territory occured during this time period. the United Kingdom acquired as colonies or protectorates the following: U.A.E. (1853); Kuwait, Oman, Qatar, and southern Arabia (1860); Bahrain (1861); Yemen (1874); Egypt and Sudan (1882); and Palestine and Transjordan (1921). In addition, the U.K. maintained naval dominance over the Indian Ocean and Persian Gulf from mid-1700 until 1971.

Due to increased nationalism and revolt, the UK signed the Anglo-Egyptian Treaty in 1936 giving more power to King Farouk, tenth ruler of the Mohammed Ali dynasty that had begun during Napoleon's invasion of Egypt. By the time of W.W.II, Britain was in Egypt mainly to keep the Suez Canal open. However, Britain remained in firm control of the Middle East-to-Far East during this time period. The United Kingdom was unquestionably *"the king of the South"*, with India as the jewel in the British Crown. In 1941, during W.W. II, the UK and Soviet forces invaded the Kingdom of Iran because Shah Reza Pahlavi had made overtures toward Nazi Germany, thus prompting the UK to secure the Iranian oil fields. Britain also took Baghdad, Iraq, during W.W. II for the same reasons. Millions living in India, the Middle East, or North Africa lived their entire lives as citizens of the United Kingdom of Great Britain without having ever seen their motherland.

Though some might argue nowadays that Great Britain's dominance of these lands was inexcusable, there is another side to that argument. The people of the Middle East and Far East during this time period were still living at a 10th century lifestyle, complete with legalized slavery, rampant poverty and disease and an illiteracy rate as high as 90%. Even as late as 1910 in the Ottoman Empire, when the legitimate heir would assume the throne, all of his male siblings of the royal household would

---

[41] Nicholas, Lynn H. (May 1995) [1994]. *The Rape of Europa: The Fate of Europe's Treasures in the Third Reich and the Second World War*. New York City: Vintage Books. ISBN 978-0-679-40069-1.

BRITISH COLONIES & DOMINIONS
In the Middle East, 1943

- Colonies
- Dominions

be summarily executed. The human rights violations inflicted upon the poorer classes were unimaginable. Beacause of this *Pax Britanica*, these vast regions of the world were now open to Christian missionaries, doctors and teachers, like the famous Dr. Livingstone of Africa, who worked tirelessly to bring an end to the wretched condition of these pitiable people and bring them the hope of the good news of Jesus Christ. }

25. And he will stir up his strength and courage against the king of the South with a large army;
Hitler stirred up his *Deutsches Afrikakorps* under Field Marshall Rommel to seize Egypt and North Africa from the U.K. For a brief while, German forces controlled almost all of North Africa including one-third of Egypt.

25. ...so the king of the South will mobilize an extremely large and mighty army for war; and he [that is, Hitler's forces] will not stand,
So the *king of the South*, Prime Minister Winston Churchill, mobilized an *"extremely large and mighty army for war"* including UK forces throughout the entire empire. Under Field Marshal Bernard Montgomery, the German forces were unable to stand and were pushed out of Egypt at the 2nd battle of El Alamein in 1942 and out of Tripoli, Libya, in 1943.

We know that this portion of the verse is referring to Hitler's army being unable to stand, by the purposeful absence of the phrase *"the king of the south"* in the last half of the verse. Remember that the *"despicable person"*, Adolph Hitler did not deserve the *"honor of kingship...conferred"* upon him. So Daniel, to maintain consistency within the prophecy, only refers to Hitler as *"he"* or *"him"*. And continuing the reference to Hitler...

25...for schemes will be devised against him
26. and they that eat of his delicate food shall break him, and his army shall be dissolved (Darby)
"Schemes" were devised against Hitler as "Operation Valkyrie", originally a Hitler-approved plan to divest power to the regional magistrates in the event of an invasion, was secretly turned into a plan of assassination and overthrow of the Nazi government. Some of Hitler's closest officers in the Wehrmacht (army), *"who eat his delicate food,"* were in on the plot including:
• Field Marshal Erwin Rommel
• Colonel Claus von Stauffenberg (who planted the bomb and was in charge of the reserve army)
• 1st Lieutenant Werner von Haeften (Stauffenberg's aid)
• Colonel Albrecht von Quirnheim
• General Friedrich Olbricht (General of the Infantry)
• Major-General Henning von Tresckow (Chief of Staff of the entire Eastern-Front Army).

In July of 1944, one month after the American-British invasion at the beaches of Normandy, Stauffenberg planted a bomb at a conference in Rastenburg. Hitler escaped with minor injuries—at least in the physical sense. The word, *"break"* here (or in NASV *"destroy"*), in Hebrew, *shäbar*, means *"to break down"* or *"to break one's mind"*.[42] After the assassination attempt, Hitler became furiously paranoid. Operation Valkyrie led to the arrest of more than 5,000 people and the execution of about 4,900 of them, and the destruction of the resistance movement. For the next nine months, Hitler would be all but invisible, making no more public appearances and hiding his travels. German General Heinz Guderian made an observation of Hitler after the assassination attempt on July 20:

"After the July 20th attempt, Hitler was a sick man... and not in complete possession of his faculties. His left side trembled. His mind was not clear enough to appreciate the real situation of Germany... He had a special picture of the world, and every fact had to fit in with that fancied picture. As he believed, so the world must be. But, in fact, it was a picture of another world."[43]

In April of 1945, Hitler committed suicide in his bunker in Berlin, but not before he flooded the city's storm sewers thereby drowning the German people who had taken refuge there from the Allied bombings. The July assassination attempt accelerated the decline and surrender of the Third Reich, quenching the ardor of the Wehrmacht and the people of Deutschland. Lacking in strong leadership, the hierarchy of the military and Nazi army quickly *"dissolved."*

26...and many will fall down slain.
"Many"—the root word here means *"multitudes"* or *"myriads"* (myriad=ten

DANIEL, CHAPTER 11:23-26

23. And after an alliance is made with him he will practice deception, and he will go up and gain power with a small force of people. 24. In a time of tranquility he will enter the richest parts of the realm and he will accomplish what his fathers never did nor his ancestors; he will distribute plunder, booty, and possessions among them and he will devise his schemes against strongholds, but only for a time. 25. And he will stir up his strength and courage against the king of the South with a large army; for schemes will be devised against him... 26. and they that eat of his delicate food shall break him, and his army shall be dissolved.

Prime Minister Winston Churchill
"...the king of the South will mobilize an extremely large and mighty army for war."

---

[42] http://cf.blueletterbible.org/lang/lexicon/lexicon.cfm?Strongs=H07665&t=kjv
[43] http://ww2db.com/person_bio.php?person_id=95

thousand) and was the largest number in Daniel's vocabulary. Accordingly, W.W.II was the most costly war to date, claiming over 70 million lives.

{ Historical Timeline: The official act of surrender of Nazi Germany took place on May 8, 1945, in the outskirts of Berlin, Germany. It was attended by representatives of GB, USA, USSR, France, and the German military.}

27. As for both kings...
The term *"both kings"* obviously refers to the kings of the north and of the south. As previously shown, at this particular time in world history the indisputable king of the South who held final authority over all others in the region was the United Kingdom of Great Britain. As has been consistently interpreted from the beginning, Daniel was specifically avoiding any racial or national connotation by use of the term *"king of the South"* (or *"...North"* for that matter).

As for the Northern kingdom, the last reference here was regarding Czarista Alexandra Fyodorovna of Russia in verse 17. Germany was never given this title, neither during Kaiser Wilhelm's reign nor especially during the Nazi Third Reich since Hitler was singled-out as not worthy of the title. Russia of course was taken over by the Bolsheviks in the October Revolution of 1917 and became the USSR, or "Soviet Union," and was initially headed by the dictator Vladimir Ilyich Lenin until just two years before his death in 1922. He was succeeded by the infamous and ruthless, Joseph Stalin—the *king of the North*.

27... their hearts will be intent on evil, and they will speak lies [to each other] at the same table; but it will not succeed...
On July 17, 1945, in Potsdam, Germany, the leaders of the four powers sat literally *"at the same table"* and signed the Allied Control Council, giving these four Allied powers authority over the German civil authority. Even as the Potsdam conference was being scheduled, Prime Minister Churchill was planning Operation Unthinkable, a plan for the UK and USA to force the USSR, by war if necessary, to relinquish territory that she had gained in Germany, Czechoslovakia, Poland, Romania, and Hungary. Truman rejected the idea as un-winnable.

Stalin, however, lived up to Churchill's low expectations: The USSR never allowed Poland the freedom of self government as they had promised, and they kept the 15% war reparations that had been promised to rebuild Poland. Though Polish forces had fought valiantly and in great numbers alongside the Allies in order to defeat the Nazis, their lands were given away to the Soviets for reasons that at the time seemed realistic and pragmatic.

27... for the end is still to come at the appointed time.
An ominous foreshadowing—but it does seem to indicate that the region comprising the Soviet Union will be involved in the "end game" at the appointed time.

28. Then he will return to his land with much plunder;
Stalin returned from the Potsdam conference with *"much plunder"* indeed! The lands and natural resources of what would become the entire Eastern Block would become Stalin's for the taking—sealed behind an Iron Curtain.

28; but his heart will be set against the holy covenant and he will take action and [then] return to his [own] land.
According to R.J. Rummel, Professor emeritus of Poly-Sci. at the University of Hawaii, more than 61 million people were executed or died during imprisonment in the Soviet gulag during the 1920's and 1930's. And according to the Oxford University Press, *World Christian Encyclopedia*, during the two decades from 1920 to 1940, 45 million of this number were Christians. The Russian Orthodox churches, numbering over 55,000 prior to the October Revolution, were reduced to less than 500 under the intense persecution of the Bolsheviks and Stalin. From 1917 to 1935, 130,000 orthodox priests were arrested and 95,000 were put to death, often tortured by the most horrific means imaginable.

29. At the appointed time he will return and come into the South, but this last time it will not turn out the way it did before.
The Soviet Union, still under the dictatorship of Stalin, came into the South in 1946—*"the appointed time"*, apparently predetermined by Providence. Stalin was attempting to subvert the governments of Turkey and Greece, where the Soviets had instigated a civil war, in order to expand the Soviet Empire. He wanted to gain unfettered egress from the Black Sea through the Dardanelles to the Mediterranean and also to set up a

DANIEL, CHAPTER 11:26-29

26...and many will fall down slain. 27. As for both kings their hearts will be intent on evil, and they will speak lies [to each other] at the same table; but it will not succeed for the end is still to come at the appointed time. 28. Then he will return to his land with much plunder; but his heart will be set against the holy covenant and he will take action and return to his land. 29. At the appointed time he will return and come into the South, but this last time it will not turn out the way it did before.

"Then he will return to his land with much plunder..."

"...they will speak lies... at the same table..."
Stalin returned from the Potsdam conference with the lands and natural resources of what would become the entire Eastern Block.

61

Soviet Naval base on one of the Turkish-controlled Dodecanese Islands of the Aegean Sea.

Because of these events, President Harry Truman of the United States, initiated and signed into law The Truman Doctrine on March 12, 1947. It stated in effect that the policy of communist containment would shift from a passive to an active stance. Economic and military aid would be funneled to the free lands whose governments were being subverted by internal, violent, communist minorities or external Soviet sedition. For Stalin, it did *"not turn out the way it did before."*

30. For ships of Kittim will come against him; therefore he will be disheartened,
The word *"Kittim"* literally refers to the island of Cyprus in the Mediterranean, but the word is always used in the plural sense in the Bible to denote a region—particularly the island regions around the Adriatic Sea (between Greece and Italy) and the Aegean Sea (between Greece and Turkey).

Since the invasion of the shores of Tripoli by the United States Marines against the Barbary Pirates in the days of President Thomas Jefferson, the U.S. 6th Fleet has maintained a presence in the Mediterranean. Headquartered in Gaeta, Italy, the 6th Fleet, which included the battleship *Missouri* (where Japan had recently signed terms of surrender) and the carrier *USS Franklin D. Roosevelt*, were on maneuvers in the Aegean and Adriatic seas at the time that Stalin was attempting to destabilize the region.
• On April 5th, anchored in the Bosporus off the coast of Istanbul, Turkey, the *Missouri* rendered full honors in the form of a 19-gun salute to honor the death of the Turkish ambassador to the U.S. This "honor" was a thinly-veiled threat meant to intimidate the Soviets.
• On April 9th, anchored off the coast of Athens, Greece, the *Missouri* and the *USS Franklin D. Roosevelt*, were greeted with an overwhelming welcome by the Greek governmental officials.

The dispatch of the 6th fleet by Truman to the eastern Mediterranean was not a coincidence, but a direct response to the Soviet threat in Turkey and Greece. Historians mark this event as the beginning of the Cold War that existed between the U.S. and the U.S.S.R. Stalin became *"disheartened"* at the turn of events and returned to Moscow to scheme again.

30...and will return and become enraged at the holy covenant and take action;
Not only in the USSR but also in her satellite Eastern Bloc nations (especially Romania, Bulgaria, and Albania) faith in Christ was considered sedition and a mental disease. Many Christians endured psychological torture and "re-education" in the KGB headquarters of Lubyanka prison in Moscow and in Pitești prison in Romania. During W.W.II, Stalin's persecution against Christians had waned a bit because Stalin needed the unifying effect of the deep, spiritual allegiances of the Russian Orthodox Church which he extorted for his own purposes. However, after his death in 1953, his successor Nikita Khrushchev fanned the flames of anti-Christian persecution with renewed ardor. The churches that had begun to be re-opened decreased from 25,000

at the beginning of Khrushchev's reign to less than 7,000 by 1985, and approximately 50,000 clergy of all denominations had been mercilessly executed.

30...so he will come back and show regard for those who forsake the holy covenant.
Not only did Khrushchev instigate overt persecution against Christians, but blatant favoritism was shown toward atheists and members of the Communist Party. The youth of the *Komsomol* (the youth wing of the Communist Party) were encouraged to vandalize churches and brutalize Christians, including the elderly and other youth. Christians were forbidden to join the Communist Party and were prevented from pursuit of prominent careers and reduced to menial jobs.

31. And forces from him will arise, desecrate the sanctuary fortress, and do away with the regular sacrifice. And they will set up the abomination of desolation.
I will refer to this in detail in Chapter 12, but for now note that there are three distinct events with many "days" between the events:
1) desecration of the sanctuary fortress
2) abolition of the regular sacrifice
3) the abomination of desolation

32. And by smooth words he will turn to godlessness those who act wickedly toward the covenant, but the people who know their God will display strength and take action.
Under Khrushchev, anti-religious propaganda was encouraged, and the church was denied any forum for public response and was forbidden to respond in print. But great men such as Pope John Paul II, Brother Andrew—the Dutchman who smuggled Bibles into Communist Europe, Pastor Richard Wurmbrand, Alexander Solzhenitsyn, and many others known only to God, displayed great strength and took action against the threat of communism.

33. And those who have insight among the people will give understanding to the many; yet they will fall by sword and by flame, by captivity and by plunder, for many days.

Here, Daniel is summarizing the many days of communist oppression that began in 1917. As a Protestant Christian, I may have some profound doctrinal differences with Russian Orthodox and Catholic believers, but I will never dishonor my Lord by questioning the faith of these devout brothers in Christ who have endured unto torture and death the malevolence and hatred of communist oppression. Men such as:
• Metropolitan Benjamin, head of the Petrograd, Orthodox Diocese. At his farce trial in 1922, he blessed all of those present including his accusers and defended others against indictment, taking upon himself full responsibility for breaking unjust and immoral laws. His last words to the judge before his execution were, *"...no matter what you decide, life or death, I will lift up my eyes reverently to God, cross myself and affirm: 'Glory to Thee, my Lord, glory to Thee for everything.'"* One of his fellow martyrs, Archimandrite Sergius prayed aloud before the firing squad, *"Forgive them, Father, for they know not what they do."* [44]
• Pope John Paul II practiced his faith for decades as a Polish priest under the hammer of communism. He spoke openly against Soviet oppression and supported the Polish *Solidarity* movement. We now know that the failed assassination attempt against him in

1981 was orchestrated by the KGB. The Pope openly forgave his attacker and met with him and his family on more than one occasion.
• Pastor Richard Wurmbrand, who spent eight-and-a-half years in a Romanian prison merely for preaching the Gospel of Christ. Three full years of this were spent in solitary confinement. He endured horrific torture at the hands of the sadistic, secret police. He was finally released in 1956 but was re-arrested in 1959 for refusing to cease preaching about Christ to members of the 'underground' church of Romania. Due to increased political pressure from Western countries (see verse 34), pastor Wurmbrand was granted amnesty and released in 1964.
• The writer, Alexander Solzhenitsyn, who spent 8 years at forced labor in the Gulag of Siberia. After being deported in 1972, he appeared before the U.S. Congress in 1975 where he testified,

"The Communist leaders say, 'Don't interfere in our internal affairs. Let us strangle our citizens in peace and quiet.' But I tell you: Interfere more and more. Interfere as much as you can. We beg you to come and interfere."[45]

And again, much to the chagrin of the Congressional Liberals, he stated,
" America... they are trying to weaken you; they are trying to disarm your strong and magnificent country..."[46]

34. Now when they fall they will be granted a little help,
Christians and others used by God in the West have done what we could to support the suffering church, oppressed by communism. Many organizations, such as Brother Andrew's, Open Doors ministry, poured in Bibles and money to victims of Soviet

"Mr. Gorbachev, tear down this wall..." challenged President Reagan, *"...they will be granted a little help..."* Pope John Paul II also spoke openly against Soviet oppression.

oppression. Political leaders like President Reagan strengthened those who were suffering by openly naming the USSR, "an evil empire" and loudly challenging General Secretary Gorbachev to "…tear down this wall!"[47]

34… and many will join with them in hypocrisy.
Throughout the 60 years of persecution at the hands of the communists, legitimate pastors and priests were replaced by KGB agents and operatives in attempts to subvert and undermine the Christian faith from within. This forced many believers to practice their faith in underground or outlawed services. Since the fall of the Soviet Union and the opening of many governmental records, the shear extent of KGB infiltration into the Orthodox Church in particular that has been revealed, is staggering.

• "It was not just one or two people. The whole church was under control…we looked at the archives."[48]
• Seeing documentary proof "left a shocking impression [that the church] was practically a subsidiary, a sister company of the KGB."[49]
• One man, in Perm-36 internment camp of the gulag worked for an elderly priest in Chita and found him to be an "atheist and a drunk."[50]
• Among the KGB agents, say those who have reviewed the archives, is the current patriarch of the Russian Church, Alexy II. One Soviet-era dissident exclaimed, "Our patriarch and our president (Putin) have the same background. They are from the same firm—the KGB."[51]

DANIEL, CHAPTER 11:30-38

30. For ships of Kittim will come against him; therefore he will be disheartened, and will return and become enraged at the holy covenant and take action so he will come back and show regard for those who forsake the holy covenant. 32. And by smooth words he will turn to godlessness those who act wickedly toward the covenant, but the people who know their God will display strength and take action. 33. And those who have insight among the people will give understanding to the many; yet they will fall by sword and by flame, by captivity and by plunder, for many days. 34. Now when they fall they will be granted a little help, and many will join with them in hypocrisy. 35. And some of those who have insight will fall, in order to refine, purge, and make them pure, until the end time; because it is still to come at the appointed time. 36. Then the king will do as he pleases, and he will exalt and magnify himself above every god, and will speak monstrous things against the God of gods; and he will prosper until the indignation is finished for that which is decreed will be done. And he will show no regard for the God of his fathers, or for the desire of women, nor will he show regard for any god; for he will magnify himself above them all. 38. But instead he will honor a god of fortresses, a god whom his fathers did not know; he will honor with gold, silver, costly stones, and treasures.

---

[44] New York Times, July 20, 1919
[45] http://humanrightsforworkers.blogspot.com/2008/08/solzhenitsyn-we-beg-you-to-interfere.html
[46] http://www.themoralliberal.com/2009/12/10/america-confront-communists-with-strength-alexander-solzhenitsyn/
[47] U.S. President Ronald W. Reagan, June 12, 1987 at the Brandenburg Gate, Berlin, Germany
[48] The Wall Street Journal, Dec.18, 2007; Putin and Orthodox Church Cement Power in Russia—Higgins.

35. And some of those who have insight will fall, in order to refine, purge, and make them pure, until the end time; because it is still to come at the appointed time.
This reference to "falling" is obviously not about martyrdom since it is difficult to be refined for service when one is not of this world anymore. Sometimes, Christians *"fall"* because of the abundance of revelation and *"insight"* given to them. Like the Apostle Paul, they are given a *"thorn in the flesh,"* a weakness if you will, in order to keep them humble and mindful of their true-human condition. The promise here for all Christians is not to give up—you are being refined for the honor of serving Christ at the end time.

36. Then the king will do as he pleases, and he will exalt and magnify himself above every god, and will speak monstrous things against the God of gods; and he will prosper until the indignation is finished for that which is decreed will be done.
Whether it be Lenin, Stalin, (or in this chronological sequence) Khrushchev or his successor Brezhnev the arrogance and audacity of Soviet leaders to praise atheistic communism and decry the worship of God as mental illness and tantamount to governmental subversion has known no bounds. The USSR did indeed prosper until the *"indignation"* was finished and *"that which [was] decreed...was done."* Communism has shown itself to be totally bankrupt as an economic or political system and as President Reagan so eloquently phrased it, assigned to *"the ash-heap of history."*[52]

37. And he will show no regard for the God of his fathers...,
The Czars considered the city of Moscow in the Empire of Russia as the 3rd Rome, replacing the Christian strongholds of Papal Rome and Constantinople. Stalin realized almost too late, that he needed the adhesive force of the Christian faith to rally the Russian army to fight for the Motherland against Nazi invasion. Atheistic communism must force obedience within its population because it is devoid of any ability to inspire loyalty and faithfulness among its subjects except within the top 1% of the Communist Party that enjoys the pleasures and advantages of totalitarianism.

37... or for the desire of women...
Communism ignored the desire of women to have and to nurture their offspring. Children became the property of the State to train and to brainwash as they deemed fitting. The maternal instinct to love and cherish their babies and toddlers was belittled as unnecessary and mere emotion. The State could not allow any other teaching or outside influence of its youth except for the approved communist indoctrination.

"Communist educators would have liked to take charge of children from the day they were born, removing them from their parents and placing them in communal nurseries. ...In 1921, Zlata Lilina, an official of the Commissariat of Enlightenment, insisted that it was best for children to be removed from their homes...'Raising children is not the private task of parents, but the task of society.'"[53]

[49-51] ibid

[52] http://www.reagansheritage.org/reagan/html/reagan_panel_pipes.shtml. In the speech, Reagan freely admits that this was authored by the communist, Trotsky, and revels in the poetic irony.

[53] *Russia under the Bolshevik Regime*, p331 by Richard Pipes ©1994

THE TRUE EVIL: THE U.S.S.R.

Civil War Killings (1917)
3,284,000 (estimated total)
Terror: 750,000
Concentration Camps: 34,000
Forced Famine: 2,500,000

New Economic Policy Killings (1923)
2,200,000 (estimated total)

Collectivization Killings (1929)
11,440,000 (estimated total)
Terror: 1,733,000
Deportation Deaths: 1,400,000
Concentration Camps: 3,306,000
Forced Famine: 5,000,000

The Great Terror Killings (1936)
4,345,000 (estimated total)
Terror: 1,000,000
Deportation Deaths: 65,000
Concentration Camps: 3,280,000

Pre- WWII (1939)
5,104,000 (estimated total)
Terror: 1,932,000
Deportation Deaths: 283,000
Concentration Camps: 2,889,000

WWII Killings (1941)
13,053,000 (estimated total)
Terror: 1,257,000
Deportation Deaths: 1,036,000
Concentration Camps: 10,761,000

Post- WWII Killings (1946)
15,613,000 (estimated total)
Terror: 1,376,000
Deportation Deaths: 1,557,000
Concentration Camps: 12,348,000

Post-Stalin Killings (1954)
6,872,000 (estimated total)
Terror: 250,000
Deportation Deaths: 8,000
Concentration Camps: 6,613,000

TOTAL KILLED = 62 MILLION (1917-1991)
Source: R.J. Rummel's "Death by Government"

This physical, spiritual, and emotional abuse took its toll on almost an entire generation of Russian children in the form of undiagnosed mental illness. What is alarming is the realization that the current leaders of Russia, both Putin and Medvedev, were reared and indoctrinated in these same, government-run, institutions.

37... nor will he show regard for any god; for he will magnify himself above them all.
Neither did communism have regard for any *"god"*, be it Christian, Muslim, Buddhist, or whatever. The State and the Communist Party reigned supreme. They were the be-all and end-all of life and death. The "masses" were the expendable worker ants that lived purely at the discretion of and for the benefit and prolongation of the Communist State.

38. But instead he will honor a god of fortresses, a god whom his fathers did not know; he will honor with gold, silver, costly stones, and treasures.
More than anything else, the Soviet economy was dedicated to military preparedness and armament. Working conditions, human rights, and benefits to its populace were not even in the top 100 concerns. People went without food and basic needs for the sake of the military. The USSR was a third-world nation with a first-rate military. At the height of the Cold War and according to Soviet publications[54], the USSR spent anywhere from 40% to 80% of its GNP to produce and maintain its conventional and nuclear arsenal and equipment. Compared to this, the United States outspent the Soviets with only 15% of our GNP at the height of President Reagan's so-called arms-race.

"...he will honor a god of fortresses... with gold, silver, costly stones, and treasures."
The U.S.S.R. spent up to 80% of its GNP on the military at the height of the Cold War.

---

[54] http://intellit.muskingum.edu/russia_folder/pcw_era/sect_05.htm

Future Events

Daniel 11:39 - 12:13

FUTURE EVENTS
"...for now we see through a glass darkly..." (1 Cor. 13:12)

{ Historical Timeline: It is my belief based upon observable data that what follows from here are current-to-future events and as such, much of what is written is speculation and prognostication on my part—db; March 2008.}

39. And he will take action against the strongest of fortresses with [the help of] a foreign god; he will cause them to rule over the many, and will parcel out land for a price.
He, that is the king of the North (Putin?), will take action against the *"strongest of fortresses"*—clearly (at least at the current time) the United States of America –a superlative term for the only "super power" in the world today. Though in a future scenario this could also apply to the "Fourth Beast" of Revelations—the Anti-Christ Empire. Russia, with *"the help of a foreign god"*, that is the so-called god of Islam, will cause the Arab and Islamic nations to rule in many places. Together, they will subvert U.S. attempts at stabilization of governments, particularly in the Middle East. Russia will even sell off huge parcels of land for the right price. Mr. Putin is the new Czar of modern Russia (unofficially of course) and has been endowed by the new Russian Church with an almost mystical right to rule indefinitely.[55]

40. And at the end time the king of the South will collide with him…
This is the beginning of the end game, or final 10-minute-warning in the Super Bowl of history. But collide with whom? Not against the king of the North—but collide against the *"strongest of fortresses,"* the United States. The forces of Islam centralized in whichever country (currently undefined unless one includes al Qaeda) will collide or more literally— *thrust* against the U.S. The picture here in Hebrew is: thrust-and-retreat; thrust-and-retreat; continuing as long as possible without actually

"And he will take action against the strongest of fortresses with [the help of] a foreign god..."
Putin of Russia meeting with President Assad of Syria.

---

[55] *The Wall Street Journal,* Dec.18, 2007; *Putin and Orthodox Church Cement Power in Russia*—Higgins.

inciting fierce retribution. And we have seen this being fulfilled in the first World Trade Center attack; attacks against US Embassies in Kenya and elsewhere; the attack against the USS Cole; and the 9-11 attacks against the WTC and the Pentagon.

40... and the king of the North will storm against him with chariots, with horsemen, and with many ships;
While the United States is busy keeping the Islamic scorpions at bay, pulling our punches so as not to hurt them badly or make them really, really angry (excuse the sarcasm), the Russian bear will use this time to strike America—and strike hard! To *"storm against"* is like a hurricane, and with everything they've got. Obviously, at our current point in time (2008) there is no provocation for such an action by the Russians, nor would it be wise—but who knows what the future may bring.

40...and he will enter countries, overflow and pass through.
The Russian military will have neither the will nor the military resources to commit troops to an occupational force. They will enter the countries (presumably the United States—possibly not, but most certainly the former Eastern Bloc countries as well as Western Europe), overwhelm their forces, and pass through. An alternative interpretation to this portion of verse 40 is that this coincides with and begins the prophecy of Ezekiel chapter 38 and the predictions regarding Gog and Magog.

41. He will also enter the Beautiful Land, and many will fall; but these will be rescued out of his hand: Edom, Moab and the foremost of the sons of Ammon.
This portion does begin to coincide with Ezekiel 38 and the invasion of Israel by Gog and Magog (Russia) and her allies. The fact that the Arab nations mentioned above are *"rescued"* out of his hand reveals the alliance between Russia and the *"king of the South"* and an implied treaty by Russia not to invade these lands. It also positively identifies Israel as the *"beautiful land"* specified here since it is in the same area geographically.

42. Then he will stretch out his hand against countries, and the land of Egypt will not escape.
The land of Egypt and the Suez Canal—Russia does not have to own the world's oil reserves, just control them. Why Egypt?—because, the country has had a long-standing peace treaty with Israel since the death of Egyptian President Nasser and the expulsion of the Soviet advisors in 1972 by President Sadat.

43. But he will gain control over the hidden treasures of gold and silver and over all the precious things of Egypt; and Libyans and Ethiopians at his footsteps.
In the biblical mind, Daniel includes here almost the entire continent of what we now call Africa. The hidden treasures in the land of Egypt. Libya, which in biblical geography also includes all the nations of north-west Africa from Morocco to the Sudan. And Ethiopia (lit. *"Cush"* in Hebrew), which includes the entire interior of Africa occupied by the indigenous black-African tribes. The inference here and in the preceding verse is that Egypt will be conquered whereas Libya and Cush, the mostly-Muslim countries, will follow willingly—presumably to garner some advantage in power, land, and wealth.

44. But rumors from the East and from the North will disturb him, and he will go forth with great wrath to destroy and annihilate many.
The *"kings of the East"* as mentioned in Revelation 16:12 will not sit idly by as Russia takes control of a vast portion of the global oil supply. The book of Revelation also tells us to expect the Euphrates River to dry up at this point in time.

> *Revelation 16:12 reads: "And the sixth angel poured out his bowl upon the great river, the Euphrates; and its water was dried up, that the way might be prepared for the kings from the rising of the sun."*

The prophet Isaiah describes a similar occurrence which also includes some event of significance happening to the Red Sea.

> *Isaiah 11:15, 16: "And the Lord will utterly destroy the tongue of the Sea of Egypt; and He will wave His hand over the River (i.e. the Euphrates) with His scorching wind; and He will strike it into seven streams, and make men walk over dry-shod. And there will be a highway from Assyria for the remnant of His people who will be left..."*

44. But rumors from the East and from the North will disturb him, and he will go forth with great wrath to destroy and annihilate many.
The *"North"* here could refer to reprisal by Great Britain or possibly a retaliatory nuclear strike over the North Pole by the United States against Russia's cities. Just what these *"rumors"* are is not defined, but obviously Russia will feel threatened by them and will retaliate with *"great wrath to destroy and annihilate many."* It is an assumption on my part again, but the veracity of the words would seem to indicate a nuclear strike of some kind by Russia.

45. And he will pitch the tents of his royal pavilion between the seas and the beautiful Holy Mountain; yet he will come to his end, and no one will help him.
...Between the Seas of the Mediterranean and either the Sea of Galilee or the Dead Sea, and the Holy Mountain in Jerusalem (or is it Mount Sinai?), the valley of Hamon-Gog as specified in Ezekiel 39. Its exact location is yet unknown, but such will be the end of the Russian Army, on the mountains of Israel.

* * * * *

These first few verses of chapter 12 are the direct fulfillment of the preface to Chapters 11 and 12 found in Daniel 10:14, when the angel told Daniel,

> *"I have come to give you an understanding of what will happen to your people in the end of the days, for the vision pertains to the days yet future."*

CHAPTER 12
1. Now at that time Michael, the great prince who stands over the sons of your people, will arise. And there will be a time of distress such as never occurred since there

*In the end times the Archangel Michael will arise and
"...there will be a time of distress such as never occured..."*

"And many of those who sleep in the dust of the ground will awake, these to everlasting life, but the others to disgrace and everlasting abhorrence." Daniel 12:2

was a nation until that time; and at that time your people, everyone who is found written in the book will be rescued.
It is after the destruction of the Russian Army that the *"time of distress"* begins that is generally believed to be the Great Tribulation Period of 3-1/2 years.

2. And many of those who sleep in the dust of the ground will awake, these to everlasting life, but the others to disgrace and everlasting abhorrence.
A reference to the return of Christ and the first resurrection of the dead. As the Apostle John related,

> *"...And I saw the souls of those who had been beheaded because of the testimony of Jesus and because of the word of God, and those who had not worshipped the beast or his image, and had not received the mark upon their forehead and upon their hand; and they came to life and reigned with Christ for a thousand years. The rest of the dead did not come to life until the thousand years were completed. This is the first resurrection. Blessed and holy is the one who has a part in the first resurrection; over these the second death has no power, but they will be priests of God and of Christ and will reign with Him for a thousand years." Rev. 20:5-7*

And possibly my favorite reference from the prophet Isaiah,

> *"And the Lord of hosts will prepare a lavish banquet for all peoples on this mountain...and on this mountain He will swallow up the covering which is over all peoples, even the veil which is stretched over all nations. He will swallow up death for all time, and the Lord God will wipe tears away from all faces and He will remove the reproach of His people from all the earth; for the Lord has spoken." Isaiah 25:6-8*

3. And those who have insight will shine brightly like the brightness of the expanse of heaven, and those who lead the many to righteousness, like the stars forever and ever.
On a moonless night, when all other lights go out, the stars are at their brightest! As the prophet Isaiah declared,

> *"Arise, shine; for your light has come, and the glory of the Lord has risen upon you. For behold, darkness will cover the earth, and deep darkness the peoples; but the Lord will rise upon you, and His glory will appear upon you. And nations will come to your light, and kings to the brightness of your rising." Isaiah 60:1-3*

4. But as for you, Daniel, conceal these words and seal up the book until the end of time; many will go back and forth, and knowledge will increase.
For over 2,200 years, the eleventh chapter of Daniel has been sealed and wrongly interpreted. But now, I humbly submit, the seal has been broken—at least, up to a point.

5. Then I, Daniel, looked and behold, two others were standing, one on this bank of the river, and the other on that bank of the river.

God protected Daniel through many circumstances where he faced certain death and spoke audibly to the prophet in many dreams and visions. God even revealed future events to Daniel by enabling him to interperet the dreams of King Nebuchadnezzar.

6. *And one said to the man dressed in linen, who was above the waters of the river, "How long until the end of wonders?"*

7. *And I heard the man dressed in linen, who was above the waters of the river, and he raised his right hand and his left toward heaven, and swore by Him who lives forever that it would be for a time, times, and half; and as soon as to finish shattering the hand of the holy people, all these will be completed.*[56]

What I propose here is of course speculation, but I submit that the *"time, times, and half a time"* written here is not the same event in the book of Revelation that is normally interpreted as 3-1/2 years, but it is nevertheless intriguing and it fits within our current time frame. I propose that the clock for the *"holy people"* initiated with the people of Israel leaving the bondage in Egypt in the year 1447 B.C. Adding 3-1/2 millennia (plus or minus) takes us to the year A.D. 2053± (3500-1447=2053). The phrase, *"time, times, and half a time"* is meant to be mysterious and unclear and so I am not predicting a date.

Additionally, *"three-and-a-half"* of anything is a rough measurement and not intended to have a high-degree of precision associated with it. So the above reference could correlate with anytime from the year 2038 to 2068, allowing for an accuracy of plus-or-minus 15 years. An additional caveat here is that the Lord says he was *"wroth with that generation,"* the ones who came out of Egypt. So maybe we need to add 40 years to the date to coincide with the next generation entering the Promised Land in the year 1407 BC (remember, it is before Christ so a later date is a smaller number), taking us to 2093. I hope not.

I know many Christians will reject this idea in part because some have an escapist-mentality and want to view the return of Christ as imminent. While others may believe that this mindset of our Lord's imminent return encourages righteous living, it also has the reverse effect of giving in to fatalism and surrender from the battles of the day. America is under attack from within and without, and if we still have 70 or even 30 years remaining then we need to be busy fighting the good fight of faith—not hunkering down waiting for the cavalry. And let us not forget the lesson from the parable of the five wise and five foolish virgins in Matthew 25,

> *"Now while the bridegroom was delaying, they all got drowsy and began to sleep."*

I have heard several well-meaning preachers confidently proclaim, "All the prophecies that need to be fulfilled for Christ's return have been fulfilled." Pardon my bluntness, but to make this statement takes an incredible amount of hubris, or naiveté, or both. The speaker makes the bold assumption that he understands absolutely 100%, every prophecy in the Bible—an opinion which I believe this book demonstrates as supremely false. We all still *"know in part"* and *"see through a glass darkly,"*[57] and

---

[56] I expound on the phrase, "shattering the hand of the holy people" in detail in my book, *The Woman and the Dragon*, so I will pass on this phrase for now.
[57] 1Cor.13:12

I certainly make no claims to the contrary regarding my certainty of the unfolding of future events. While the experts may question the wisdom of such honest confession for selling books, it is these self-same experts that have predicted Christ's return throughout numerous events in the past 40 years of my Christian walk—from The *Late Great Planet Earth,* written in 1970, to predictions of His return coinciding with the planetary alignment in 1981, and to the book conveniently titled, *88 Reasons Christ is Returning in 1988*, etc.

After the disappointment of Christ's non-return in 1978 and the realization that I would indeed have to actually decide on a career for my life, I determined in my mind never again to believe the so-called experts. Fool me once, shame on you. Fool me a half-dozen times means I am an incurably, naive fool.

8. As for me, I heard but could not understand; so I said, "My lord, what [will be] the final end of these?"
9. And he said, "Go Daniel, for [these] words are concealed and sealed up until the end time.

As I argued at the beginning of this book, Jerome could not possibly have known the correct interpretation to these chapters for they were still sealed up until the end time. The fact that the past and current experts have ignored this rather salient piece of scripture for 1,700 years I find to be rather troubling.

10. Many will be purged, made white and refined; but the wicked will act wickedly, and none of the wicked will understand, but those who have insight will understand.

At some future point in time even these later verses will become clearer and we shall no longer see them through a darkened glass. This seems to give some credence to the possibility that we have a few years yet to endure, since there is still some question as to the fulfillment of the following verses. Also, the words *"purged"* and *"refined"* seem to have the ominous ring of suffering and persecution attached to them. When our time comes, will we count it joy that we have been considered worthy to suffer for His name's sake?

11. And from the time that the regular sacrifice is abolished, and the abomination of desolation is set up, there will be 1,290 days.
12. How blessed is he who keeps waiting and attains to the 1,335 days!

From chapter 11 we read that *"forces... will arise"* from Russia and will be responsible for these events, and that these are the last two of three such events that were prophesied in Daniel 11:31. These three events are:

    1. *desecration of the sanctuary fortress*
        • *then an unspecified number of "days" to the next event*
    2. *abolition of the regular sacrifice*
        • *then 1,290 "days" to the next event*
    3. *the abomination of desolation*
        • *then an additional 45 "days" here until the blessed event—presumably the return of Christ*

The Hebrew word here translated as *"days"* is also translated elsewhere in the Bible as *"times"* or even *"years"*. Given the fact that this part of the prophecy was specifically singled out as a mystery, we can justifiably interpret these not to be literal, 24-hour days, but some other significant division of time like weeks, months, years, or decades. Also, since Jesus told us in Matthew 24 that *"...no man knows the hour or the day..."* when Christ shall return, it would violate this principle if the 1,335 days from the second event, *"the regular sacrifice is abolished,"* were to be taken literally. So how do we interpret the mystery of these events?

The last event seems to be agreed to be a repeat of the temple desecration in Jerusalem and so necessitates the rebuilding of the temple. Of course this cannot happen until the twin Islamic shrines of the Dome of the Rock and the Al-Aqsa Mosque are demolished from the Temple Mount. Since Russia will *"enter the beautiful land"* of Israel as foretold by Ezekiel, it seems consistent that Russia is the one who will desecrate the Holy of Holies in the Temple.

What of the other two events—how are they to be interpreted? Since chapter 11 makes it clear that the king of the North (Russia) is the one guilty of these transgressions, is there anything in Russian or Soviet history that fits the interpretation?

For the first incident, I submit the following possibility for the *"desecration of the sanctuary fortress."* It is the word *"fortress"* that is intriguing. Jerusalem has not been a fortress since the year A.D. 1271, nor is it likely to become a fortress in the near future. However, in Red Square across from St. Basil's Cathedral is a structure that means "fortress" in the Russian tongue—the Kremlin. Originally built as a defense fortress on the Moskva River, the multi-towered walls in the city of Moscow were built around the Kazan Cathedral which commemorated the city's liberation from its Polish oppressors in 1612. Then, the city of Moscow became the seat of Eastern Orthodox Christianity. In the early 1930's, Stalin had the Kazan Cathedral and the Resurrection Gates demolished to allow military parades down Red Square. In fact, a public toilet was installed on a portion of the site once held by the Kazan Cathedral. Also demolished inside the "sanctuary fortress" for the sake of the Communists were the 16th century, Chudov Monastery, the Ascension Convent, and the Savior Cathedral.

So, *"desecration of the sanctuary fortress,"* was literally fulfilled in this historical event. The fact that this sanctuary fortress was located in Moscow and not Jerusalem as previously presumed is merely that—a presumption. Likewise, the traditionalists presume that Daniel is referring to the Jewish *"sanctuary,"* but again there is nothing in the passage that would confirm this assumption. The Hebrew word here for *"sanctuary,"* is *miq-dash*, and is from the root word, *qa-dash*, which means, *" to be set apart; consecrated; holy."* Thus, a *"sanctuary"* is merely a location that is set apart as any place of worship and it is not required that it refer to the Temple in Jerusalem.

The second phrase is normally translated, *"abolition of the regular [sacrifice]"* or some similar phrase. What is odd about the translation is the lack of the Hebrew word for *"sacrifice,"* hence the reason for the word being in brackets in most translations. The literal translation for the phrase, which appears both in Daniel 11:31 and in 12:11, is, *"the removal (or abolition) of the continuance."* The word for continuance, *tamiyd*, means, *"perpetuity, continuance, evermore."* That is, it is something that is done without ceasing. I believe that what Daniel is referring to here, ties into the verse regarding the *"little horn"* of Daniel chapter 7, whom most regard as a synonymous reference for the anti-Christ. For the angel explained to Daniel,

"And he will speak out against the Most High and wear down the saints of the Highest One, and he will intend to make alterations in times and in law (decree)" Daniel 7:25

Every day, every minute, for perpetuity, the Enemy of the true God is reminded of the incarnation of God in the person of Jesus Christ. Our calendars are dated, *Anno Domini,* or *"the year of our Lord."* Every year, we celebrate His birth, death, and resurrection, and it is a source of perpetual torment of remembrance to the enemies of God. The *"little horn"*, or anti-Christ will *"intend to make alterations in times and in decree."* He will do this by attempting to abolish "the continual" reminder of our calendar system, not only of the holy-days, but the reckoning of years themselves. This attempt is not without precedent in history. For, in France in 1791, the National Constituent Assembly completed the draft of France's version of the constitution, based on humanism rather than upon the Judeo-Christian faith as was done in America.

"To make their outlook clear, the French changed the calendar and called 1792 the 'year one,' and destroyed many of the things of the past, even suggesting the destruction of the cathedral at Chartres. They proclaimed the goddess of Reason in Notre-Dame Cathedral in Paris and in other churches in France...In Paris, the goddess was personified by an actress...carried shoulder-high into the cathedral by men dressed in Roman costumes."[58]

In less than a year, the Declaration of the Rights of Man, based upon humanist thought would prove unworthy of the parchment upon which it was written. In September of 1792, the unquenchable thirst of the guillotine would become evident with the execution of some 1,300 prisoners. Before it was all over, more than 40,000 people would be decapitated in the bloody French Revolution.

And so, returning to the prophecy in Daniel, if my interpretation is true, we should see another attempt to restructure the calendar—only this time it will be a world-wide attempt. From this event until the last event of the three, when *"the abomination of desolation is set up"* will be 1,290 days. Again, I ask the question, do we look for literal days or for some other measure of time? These are merely some possible interpretations to these future events and since I am a teacher of the past and not a prophet, I will leave the interpretation of future events to others who consider themselves more eminently qualified in such matters. However, my instincts, based upon history, tell me that we will all be somewhat surprised as to how all of this unfolds.

13. But as for you, go your way to the end; then you will enter into rest and rise for your allotted portion at the end of the days.
One cannot help but to admire the character of Daniel, who, after being told in numerous visions of the coming of Messiah, the future outcome of his people, and how the history of the world's empires will conclude, he is told merely to *"go your way..."*

What a remarkable man indeed…

---

[58] How Should We Then Live? The Rise and Decline of Western Thought and Culture; 1976 Francis A. Schaeffer; Fleming H. Revell Company

The prophet Daniel, a remarkable man indeed...

Parting Comments

TO THE SKEPTIC, I POSE THIS QUESTION:

Almost 3,500 years ago, Moses cried out to the Children of Israel, "Hear, oh Israel: the Lord is our God. The Lord is One." The word, "One" (Hebrew, ĕch-hăd) is not only a testament to the Trinitarian nature of God, but in its literal translation means, "unique." I have expounded here upon 108 separate, prophetic statements—all fulfilled with 100% historical accuracy, written by a prophet who lived over 2,500 years ago. God says through the Old Testament prophet, Isaiah, "'Come now, and let us reason together,' says the Lord..." (Isaiah 1:18). Reason and logic demand an intellectually honest answer from you. Though logically, the chance fulfillment of 108 sequential and cataclysmic events approaches the infinitely small, do you dismiss these 108 fulfillments as fortuitous happenstance and ponder the "luck" of the prophet? Or do you acknowledge the uniqueness of the One True God? A uniqueness found only in the God of the Bible and the One who sees all eternity at a glance. There is no one like our God. There is none like Jehovah!

You have searched all of your life for the answers and have come up short. God respects your human will, and He will not violate that sacred independence and inalienable right granted to you as a subject of His benevolent hand. Though He will not oblige Himself to any mortal demand for incontrovertible proof, He does offer evidence to the willing and open heart. So, in all your lifelong questioning—what is the Lord's answer to you here?

TO THE PATRIOT, I MAKE THIS PROMISE:

Since chapters 11 and 12 of the book of Daniel center upon the history and conflicts between Europe and the Middle East, America's part in this unfolding drama was merely a cameo appearance at the end of the story. In the near future, however, you will be thrilled and amazed when the prophetic curtain is raised to reveal that most noble of nations on center stage—the United States of America. It has been my privelege to present these insights from the book of Daniel and I am honored that you have taken the time to read and absorb this book. Join me in my next publication, *The Chronicles of Babylon*, and visit us on the web at; *www.patriotpassion.com*.

May God continue to bless and purify America,

Daniel Bilbro

APPENDIX
A CRITICAL ANALYSIS OF THE TRADITIONAL INTERPRETATION VS. HISTORY

As described at the beginning of this book, by my count there are 108 historical events enumerated in the 36 relevant verses of Daniel chapter 11. We can quantify the degree of accuracy of certain commentators by assigning a maximum of 5 points to each of these 108 ± events. Therefore, a full interpretational rendering of all 108 events can have a possible score of 540 points (108 x 5 = 540). Of course, dividing their score by the total possible points gives a percentage grade and by definition a letter grade of A, B, C, D, or F. This process is intended to be ruthlessly objective even if my assessments are admittedly subjective. The reader is of course welcome to disagree with my subjective assessments of the traditionalists' comments and personally determine a higher or lower score. The point of this exercise is to accomplish two tasks:
1. Hold the commentator's feet to the fire and make certain that they have matched history with each and every one of the prophetic items. No points are awarded for irrelevant comments no matter how enlightening they might be in another venue.
2. Assign quantitative values to each historical event that supposedly mirrors the prophetic interpretation by a particular commentator.

Here is a list of the rules that I used for the analysis:
• If the commentator dismisses or ignores a particular phrase or event all together, they get a score of "0" for that event.
• Likewise if the translation is changed for the sake of the interpretation it also scores a "0".
• If the translated word or condition is questionable, that is an "either/or" situation, then the commentator is awarded a number between one-and-four depending upon the strength of the interpretation (i.e. how accurately does history unfold when compared to the literal meaning of the translation?).
• If the commentator does not maintain consistency in interpretation for a particular phrase, points will be deducted for the subsequent event(s) unless a logical reason is given for the change.

[Please note: it should come as no surprise that the commentaries are expressly protected by copyright laws. So except for the works of Jameison, Fauset & Brown (who have been dead for over 100 years) I am prevented from reproducing lengthy, albeit abridged, copies of their works. The reader may access the commentaries at blueletterbible.org unless noted otherwise.]

How did they score?

• Jerome (342) — I excuse Jerome since 95+% of the true history of Daniel 11 had not happened yet. Jerome's sign posts for the true interpretation would have ended at verse 6. Clearly, he did not have enough fulfillments to discern a pattern. His commentary is available online at *http://www.tertullian.org/fathers/jerome_daniel_02_text.htm*
• Sir Isaac Newton (1704) —Sir Isaac tended to ramble too much in irrelevant history. Since he was a contemporary of Matthew Henry and held to the traditional view, I did not review his commentary in detail.
• Matthew Henry (1714)—I skimmed his commentary but was convinced that J.F. & B. used his work for the basis of their own. I did not grade Henry's work, but it doubtless would score less than J.F. & B. as explained next.

- Jameison, Fauset & Brown (1871)[59] —a score of 54% graded on a curve of 96 items (explained in the following table). I used theirs because it seemed to go into more explanation and detail than did Henry. Where Henry seemed to ignore some of the details, J.F. & B. at least attempted to address more of the issues.

Sir Newton and Dr. Henry lived prior to the fulfillment of verse 12 and the rise of Napoleon, so they also could not have been expected to accurately interpret Daniel 11. However, their willing acceptance of the traditional interpretation shows how even the most critical of thinkers among us, like Isaac Newton, can be persuaded to read meaning into prophecy and thus distort the text and history in order to see that which they desire to see. It is ironic indeed coming from Newton who eschewed such conjecturing. In recently released papers authored by Newton, he estimated Christ's return to come no sooner than 2060, saying:

"This I mention not to assert when the time of the end shall be, but to put a stop to the rash conjectures of fanciful men who are frequently predicting the time of the end, and by doing so bring the sacred prophesies into discredit as often as their predictions fail."[60]

The farther we travel forward in time, the more we should expect the commentators to reevaluate the Traditional Interpretation with a more critical eye. By the time Jameison, Fauset & Brown wrote their commentary in 1871, Czarist Russia was at the height of its power and prestige and the hellish philosophy of Marxism was gaining acceptance within radical, atheistic, Jewry and Eastern Europe, thus fulfilling chapter 11 of Daniel through the first half of verse 14. Still, there were not many benchmarks to point the way to the correct interpretation, but we are rapidly getting there…

- John F. Walvoord (1971)[61] —a score of 59% (graded on 104 items in the following tables) though he disagrees with J.F. &B. in certain places.
- Pastor Chuck Smith (2000)—scored less than J.F. &B. and Walvoord for ignoring several salient points. His commentary is a verbatim transcript of a sermon and so it would be unfair to grade him against the same standard as an expositional commentary. However, if he did have more correlations between prophecy and historical events we can logically assume that he would have mentioned them in the sermon. Based on the transcript he would score an approximate 50%.
- Pastor Jon Courson (2006)[62] —the forward to his commentary written by Chuck Smith states,

"Most [commentaries] are expositional or exegetical; and they often seek to be so exacting with respect to the letter of the law, or the possible meaning of a particular word, that they lack life and inspiration…"

Though I obviously don't agree with Pastor Chuck's conclusion, I do agree with his disclaimer. Courson's commentary is written in an inspirational vein and not intended to be rigorous or thorough. However, based on a review of the commentary, he too would score approximately 50% accuracy for disregarding many relevant points.

---

[59] Jamieson, Robert; A.R. Fausset; and David Brown. "Commentary on Daniel 11." . Blue Letter Bible. 19 Feb 2000. 2009. 16 Nov 2009. <http://www.blueletterbible.org/commentaries/comm_view.cfm?AuthorID=7&contentID=2752&commInfo=6&topic=Daniel&ar=Dan_11_1 >

[60] "Papers Show Isaac Newton's Religious Side, Predict Date of Apocalypse". The Associated Press. 6-19-07

[61] Daniel—the Key to Prophetic Revelation, 1971, Moody Bible Institute

[62] Jon Courson's Application Commentary—Vol.2; 2006,Thomas Nelson Publishing

Daniel Chapter 11—Comments on the Commentary* of JAMEISON, FAUSET & BROWN

blueletterbible.org

Verse Number	Scriptural Portion-NASB	JFB Score	JFB Comment	My Comment
2	And now I will tell you the truth. Behold, three more kings are going to arise in Persia.	5	Cambyses, Smerids, and Darius	I agree
	Then a fourth will gain for more riches than all of them	5	King Xerxes, the Ahasuerus of Esther.	I agree
	as soon as he becomes strong through his riches, he will arouse the whole empire against the realm of Greece.	5	King Xerxes invasion of Greece in 480 B.C.	I agree
3	And a mighty king will arise, and he will rule with great authority and do as he pleases	5	Alexander the Great of Greece	I agree
4	But as soon as he has arisen,	0	[No comment here by JFB]	No points
	his kingdom will be broken up and parceled out toward the four winds of the heaven	5	The fourfold division of Alexander's kingdom at his death after the battle of Ipsus, 301 B.C..	I agree--the four generals of Alexander the Great
	though not to his own descendants,	5	Alexander's two sons, Heracles and Alexander IV	I agree--not to his only heir, Alexander IV. Heracles, is also another possible son from a mistress but this is disputed.
	nor according to his authority which he wielded	5	…nor according to his dominion--None of his successors had so wide a dominion as Alexander himself.	I agree

85

	for his sovereignty will be uprooted and given to others besides these.	1	Rather, besides the four successors to the four chief divisions of the empire, there will be other lesser chiefs who shall appropriate smaller fragments of the Macedonian empire [JEROME].	Quoting Jerome here, JFB agrees that it is not the children of Alexander. However, he (presumably) limits the division to the "lesser chiefs" of the Macedonian fragment--northern Greece only and the kingdom of Cassander who failed to maintain his control. However, the remaining 90% of the empire remained in firm control of the Seleucid and Ptolemy kingdoms.
5	*Then the king of the South*	0	Here the prophet leaves Asia and Greece and takes up Egypt and Syria, these being in continual conflict under Alexander's successors, entailing misery on Judea, which lay between the two. Holy Scripture handles external history only so far as it is connected with God's people, Israel [JEROME].	JFB fail to explain why Daniel would use an enigmatic phrase. There is no mention as yet of the king of the North yet JFB seems to believe that their presence is implied. JFB quotes Jerome here without defending the statement.
		3	king of . . . south--literally, "of midday": Egypt (Dan 11:8, 42), PTOLEMY Soter, son of Lagus. He took the title "king," whereas Lagus was but "governor."	Yes, but Lagus was "but 'governor' " over a portion of Macedonia--not of Egypt. Why would his son be called the "king" over the South? He identifies Ptolemy I Soter as the king of the south here--partial credit.
	will grow strong along with one of his princes	0	[This was addressed in Part 1 in great detail]	He identifies Seleucus I Nicator, a king of equal standing, as "one of his princes." Also, he fails to identify who the other "princes" were who had apparent equal standing with Seleucus.
	who will gain ascendancy over him and obtain a great dominion	3	[This was addressed in Part 1 in great detail]	"Seleucid shall be strong above Ptolemy" For the most part, yes. But the Seleucid kingdom never totally dominated the Ptolemy kingdom.
	his domain will be a great (vast) dominion indeed.	0		No attempt at an explanation here at all by JFB.
6	*And after some years (lit. "…in the end of years…")*	5	when the predicted time shall be consummated	Okay

	they will form an alliance (lit. "Join themselves together"), and the daughter of the king of the South will come to the king of the North to carry out a peaceful arrangement.	3	The king of the North, that is Syria, gave his sister Berenice to Antiochus, who thereupon divorced his former wife, Laodice, and disinherited her son, Seleucus Callinicus.	True, there was an alliance formed by the marriage. But the biblical passage indicates that the arrangement was instigated by the daughter--not by her brother, the king.
	But she will not retain her position of power, nor will he remain with his power	2	She shall not be able to effect the purpose of the alliance, namely, that she should be the mainstay of peace.	Partial credit: Berenice had no power. She was the unwilling pawn in the marriage to Antiochus II. No explanation for, "...nor will he remain with his power."
	but she will be given up, along with those who brought her in	5	"given up"... to be understood of giving up to death	True, Bernice was murdered by the jealous ex-wife, Laodice.
	and the one who sired her (HNV- "became a father to her"),	0	"...he that begat her"-- rather as Margin, "the child whom she brought forth" [EWALD].	Because they can find no "father" figure here JFB rewrite the translation here, agreeing with Ewald. An obvious case of rewriting the translation to fit the history.
	as well as he who supported her in those times.	1	Ptolemy died a natural death, "given up" is not in his case, as in Berenice's, to be understood of giving up to death, but in a general sense, of his plan proving abortive.	Inconsistency in interpretation. In the case of Bernice, "given-up"= death. In the case of Ptolemy, "given-up" = failure to achieve his goals. Ludicrous!
7	*But one of her branch of her roots*	3	. a branch of her roots . . . in his estate--Ptolemy Euergetes, brother of Berenice, succeeding in the place (Margin) of Philadelphus, avenged her death by overrunning Syria, even to the Euphrates	Technically a brother IS a branch out of the same roots as Berenice, but the passage seems to imply a familial connection that is far, more distant. Why not just say "her brother"?
	will arise in his place	5	[same as above--db]	Prince Ptolemy III becomes "king" of Egypt.

	and he will come against their army and enter the fortress (or "place of strength") of the king of the North and he will deal with them and display great strength.	5	Ptolemy Euergetes... avenged her death by overrunning Syria, even to the Euphrates.	Ptolemy III invades Syria, occupies Antioch, and even reaches Babylon. This was the height of Ptolemaic power--and its greatest extent. This was the "Third Syrian War." One wonders why Daniel does not mention the first two.
8	*And also their gods with their metal images and their precious vessels of silver and gold he will take into captivity to Egypt,*	5	Ptolemy, on hearing of a sedition in Egypt, returned with forty thousand talents of silver, precious vessels, and twenty-four hundred images, including Egyptian idols, which Cambyses had carried from Egypt into Persia. The idolatrous Egyptians were so gratified, that they named him Euergetes, or "benefactor."	Ptolemy returned the gold and images that were once stolen from Egypt by Cambyses of the previous Persian empire.
	and he on his part will refrain from attacking the king of the North for some years.	5	"Then he for several years shall desist from (contending with) the king of the north"	Quoting Mauer's translation, okay.
9	*Then the latter will enter the realm of the king of the South, but will return to his own land.*	0	come into his kingdom--Egypt: not only with impunity, but with great spoil.	It is obvious from 8b. that "the latter" (vs.9) is the king of the north who enters the realm of the king of the south. Translations support this 10-to-3. But JFB forces it to say that 'the king of the south is coming into his own kingdom—with great spoil.'
10	*And his sons will mobilize and assemble a multitude of great forces...*	3	his sons--the two sons of the king of the north, Seleucus Callinicus, upon his death by a fall from his horse, namely, Seleucus Ceraunus and Antiochus the Great.	JFB makes a "fast switch" here—from south-to-north. If the reference is to the king of the south (it isn't), then the sons can't be sons of the north! Here, I Ignore verse nine and give partial credit for verse ten.

	...and one of them will keep coming and overflow and pass through, that he may again wage war up to his very fortress.	0	one shall . . . come-- Ceraunus having died, Antiochus alone prosecuted the war with Ptolemy Philopater, Euergetes' son, until he had recovered all the parts of Syria subjugated by Euergetes. [From subsequent comments JFB makes it clear that this refers to the Battle of Raphia in 217 BC.—db]	"…one of them…"one of whom? Per JFB, one of the sons of the king of the north shall "keep coming." However, this Battle of Raphia was started, not by the Seleucid's of the north, but by Ptolemy Philopater of the south.
11	And the king of the South will be enraged and go forth and fight with the king of the North.	5	[summary--Angered at his great losses, Philopater launches an attack against Syria--db]	Okay
	Then the latter will raise a great multitude,	5	Antiochus, king of Syria, whose force was 70,000 infantry and 5000 cavalry.	Okay
	but that multitude will be given into the hand of the former.	5	into Ptolemy's hands 10,000 of Antiochus' army were slain, and 4,000 made captives.	The forces of Antiochus III were defeated by the Egyptians at Raphia. Antiochus escapes.
12	When the multitude is carried away, his heart will be lifted up, and he will cause tens of thousands to fall	3	instead of following up his victory by making himself master of the whole of Syria, as he might, he made peace with Antiochus, and gave himself up to licentiousness	Not a word about "cause tens of thousands to fall." Partial credit
	yet he will not prevail.	0	He [Philopater] shall lose the power gained by his victory through his luxurious indolence.	He believes that it is the self indulgence of Philopater that caused him not to pursue his advantage here-- thus he was not "strengthened by it." However, 8 other translations (including the NKJV) translate this as "he will not prevail." Indicating that even though his army was triumphant, he himself was defeated. Also, in contrasting his interpretation of this verse to actual history, Philopater DID prevail at the battle of Raphia. So much so that Antiochus withdrew from Judea all the way north to Lebanon.

13	*For the king of the North will again raise a greater multitude than the former,*	5	return--renew the war.	Ptolemy IV dies and Ptolemy V Epiphanes gains the throne at the age of five. Antiochus III rebuilds his army. He invades Coele-Syria and begins the 5th Syrian War.
	and at the end of the times	3	fourteen years after his defeat at Raphia.	JFB makes no comment here, "certain years" (KJV) here would have been 18 years since the Battle of Raphia. However, the literal meaning is "at the end time of the times [even of] years." It means at the end of an epoch or event or at the end of a fixed unit of time such as decade, century, etc.
	he will press on with a great army and much equipment.	4	no specific comment here by JFB. Merely a generalization for the whole verse.	Antiochus III retakes Syria and Phoenicia.
14	*Now in those times many will rise up against the king of the South*	5	Philip, king of Macedon, and rebels in Egypt itself, combined with Antiochus against Ptolemy.	Correct
	the violent ones among your people will also lift themselves up in order to fulfill the vision,	0	**[This was addressed in Part 1 in great detail]**	*Here, he interprets this as: '...the violent ones will lift themselves up which will inadvertently have the future effect of fulfilling the vision of the Jewish affliction yet to come under Antiochus Epiphanes.' I believe that this is quite a stretch from the intended meaning of: 'the violent ones will lift themselves up in order that they might cause their own vision for the Jewish people to become fulfilled.'*
	but they will fall down.	0	**[This was addressed in Part 1 in great detail]**	No explanation here by JFB. But continuing his interpretation: if they were not successful in fulfilling the vision (i.e. they "fall down" in their attempt) does this mean that the Jewish affliction would not take place? Which it obviously did.

15	*Then the king of the North will come, cast up a siege mound,*	0	king of . . . north--Antiochus the Great. take . . . fenced cities--Scopas, the Egyptian general, met Antiochus at Paneas, near the sources of the Jordan, and was defeated, and fled to Sidon, a strongly "fenced city," where he was forced to surrender.	Though correct about a battle fought at Paneas, there was no "well fortified city" there. Nor did Antiochus "cast up a siege mound" to capture the non-existing city. The battle of Paneas was between two, predominantly cavalry units—out in the open. The fact that Scopas fled to a city after the battle was over is irrelevant.
	and capture a well fortified city	0	[same as above--db]	Though Scopus fled to Sidon where he was finally captured, the battle was well over by then and Antiochus already had control of Phoenicia and the port of Sidon.
	and the forces of the South will not stand their ground, not even their choicest troops, for there will be no strength to make a stand.	2	Egypt's choicest army was sent under Eropus, Menocles, and Damoxenus, to deliver Scopas, but in vain [JEROME].	His interpretation here is the unsuccessful attempt by three Egyptian leaders to rescue Scopas from Sidon. However, this was a rescue attempt--'standing their ground' was not even possible since they had lost their ground.
16	*But he who comes against him will do as he pleases,*	0	Antiochus coming against Ptolemy Epiphanes.	JFB explains this as a repeat of the previous verse. Once is not enough?
	and no one will be able to withstand him	0	[No comment here by JFB]	No points
	he will stay for a time in the beautiful land,	5	Judea	Okay
	by which his hand shall be consumed.	0	[go to website, too long to quote here--db]	JFB give four possible interpretations here by four different authors Josephus, Lengkerke, Grotius, and Tregelles. Apparently JFB could not decide on any of them as fitting the verse, and I would agree that the meanings twist the scripture beyond logical recognition.

17	*And he will set his face to come with the power of his whole kingdom,*	0	Antiochus's purpose was, however, turned from open assault to wile, by his war with the Romans…	JFB stand this on its head. He was unable to come with the power of his whole kingdom because of the Romans so he resorts to "wile."
	bringing with him an equitable arrangement which he will put into effect	0	[KJV trans. "and upright ones with him." I prefer the NASB at left, however, JFB even interprets the KJV "upright ones" as an epithet made in sarcasm.--db]	No points for interpreting a KJV phrase as sarcasm.
	he will also give him the daughter of women	5	he gives to Ptolemy Epiphanes his daughter Cleopatra in marriage, promising Coelo-Syria and Judea as a dowry, thus securing his neutrality in the war with Rome	He gives his daughter Cleopatra I Syra (not the famous one--she was the 7th) to Ptolemy V Epiphanes
	but she will be ruined by it.	0	[No comment here by JFB]	No points
	But she will not take a stand for him or be on his side.	5	but Cleopatra favored her husband rather than her father, and so defeated his scheme [JEROME]. "She shall not stand on his side."	She always sided with her young, 16-year-old, husband, Ptolemy V.
18	*Then he will turn his face to the coastlands and capture many.*	0	He "took many" of the isles in the Aegean in his war with the Romans, and crossed the Hellespont.	*Antiochus does attempt to recapture Greece but is NOT successful. He does not "capture many." Historically inaccurate--no points.*
	But a commander will put a stop to his scorn against him	5	[we agree, see my summary to the right]	He is stopped by the Roman general Scipio. Antiochus had shown contempt for Rome's ambassadors.
	moreover, he will repay him for his scorn.	3	without his own reproach--with untarnished reputation. [The KJV here is a bit unclear. Not sure what JFB's point is either]	He is defeated by Scipio. After the battle of Magnesia, he signs the Treaty of Apamea, promising never to return to Europe among other conditions.

19	*So he will turn his face toward the fortresses of his own land,*	5	Compelled by Rome to relinquish all his territory west of the Taurus, and defray the expenses of the war, he garrisoned the cities left to him.	Okay
	but he will stumble and fall and be found no more.	1	Attempting to plunder the temple of Jupiter at Elymais by night...he was slain with his soldiers in an insurrection of the inhabitants	I can't agree that being murdered in an insurrection along with his soldiers should be phrased "stumble and be found no more." Wouldn't Daniel be consistent with a previous term, "given up" or even "broken?"
20	*Then in his place one will arise who will send a tax collector through the jewel of his kingdom*	5	[we agree, see my summary to the right]	Seleucus IV Philopater replaces Antiochus III. He is forced to raise taxes for Rome.
	yet within a few days he will be broken, though neither in anger nor in battle.	2	after a reign of 12 years...neither in anger, nor in battle-- not in a popular outbreak, nor in open battle.	JFB is stating that Heliodorus poisoned Seleucus to gain the throne—but apparently he was not "angry" when he murdered him. So according to JFB cold, calculated, murder is sufficient here to fulfill this prophecy.
21	*And in his place a despicable person will arise,*	5	[This was addressed in Part 1 in great detail]	The rise of Antiochus IV Epiphanes--the despicable ruler because of verse 31. However, one fact of history seems to belie his title regarding the Jews, Epiphanes paid for the Septuagint Translation of the Hebrew Scriptures into Greek.
	on whom the honor of kingship has not been conferred,	2	[This was addressed in Part 1 in great detail]	JFB and others claim that Epiphanes "seized the throne rather than obtaining it honorably", as if this was something new:
	but he will come in a time of tranquility and seize the kingdom by intrigue.	5	[This was addressed in Part 1 in great detail]	Epiphanes did seize the kingdom by intrigue, deception, and murder--just like his ancestors.

22	And the overflowing forces	0	[No comment here by JFB]	JFB fails to identify any "overflowing" forces. The most powerful army at the time was Rome and Epiphanes was not foolhardy enough to challenge them.
	will be flooded away before him and shattered,	2	Antiochus Epiphanes shall invade Egypt with overwhelming forces.	Epiphanes has some skirmishes with the Ptolemies, now a vassal state of Rome. He is forced to treat them with kid-gloves to keep from inciting wrath from Rome. "Shattered"---hardly.
	and also the prince of the covenant.	5	Ptolemy Philometer, the son of Cleopatra, Antiochus' sister, who was joined in covenant with him.	Okay
23	And after an alliance is made with him he will practice deception	0	[JFB fail to describe any alliance. Ptolemy is captured in battle--not by deception as JFB claim--db]	JFB (and history) fail to define or record any alliances that he made with other nations. He invades Egypt twice and captures the young Ptolemy, allowing him to reign as puppet king for the sake of Rome.
	and he will go up and gain power with a small force of people.	0	At first, to throw off suspicion, his forces were small.	There is no historical evidence of this. He invaded Egypt with an army necessary to conquer.
24	In a time of tranquility	3	literally, "unexpectedly" under the guise of friendship he seized Ptolemy Philometer.	Ptolemy was planning on attacking Epiphanes, but getting wind of the plans, Epiphanes attacked first. It was unexpected, but there was no guise of friendship--a truce possibly.
	he will enter [fall upon] the richest parts of the realm,	5	[JFB interpret this as a continuation of verse 22. The "richest parts" being Memphis and Egypt up to Alexandria--db.]	Okay
	and he will accomplish what his fathers never did, nor his ancestors	5	His predecessors, kings of Syria, had always coveted Egypt, but in vain: he alone made himself master of it.	Okay
	he will distribute plunder, booty, and possessions among them,	5	among his followers (1 Maccabees 1:19).	Okay

	and he will devise his schemes against strongholds, but only for a time.	5	He shall form a studied scheme for making himself master of the Egyptian fortresses. He gained them all except Alexandria, which successfully resisted him.	Okay
25	*And he will stir up his strength and courage against the king of the South with a large army*	0	A fuller detail of what was summarily stated (Dan 11:22-24). This is the first of Antiochus' three (Dan 11:29) open invasions of Egypt.	Apparently having run out of additional battles, JFB claim that Daniel will now go into even greater detail about prior events (as if they were not detailed enough in the first account).
	so the king of the South will mobilize an extremely large and mighty army for war	0	[No comment here by JFB]	No points
	but he will not stand, for schemes will be devised against him.	3	Philometer was defeated...they shall forecast, &c.--His own nobles shall frame treacherous "devices" against him (see Dan 11:26) [and] maladministered his affairs.	Ptolemy did not stand--he was captured. There is no record of schemes being devised against him. "Maladministered...affairs" could be construed as incompetence but not schemes.
26	*And those who eat his choice food will break him,*	1	those from whom he might naturally have looked for help, his intimates and dependents	So how did these "intimates and dependents" break Philometer? No comment by JFB. Partial credit.
	and his army will be swept away	5	[we agree, see my summary to the right]	Ptolemy's army offered little resistance.
	and many will fall down slain.	1	many shall fall down slain--(1 Maccabees 1:18, "many fell wounded to death"). Antiochus, when he might have slain all in the battle near Pelusium, rode around and ordered the enemy to be taken alive, the fruit of which policy was, he soon gained Pelusium and all Egypt	So according to JF&B they didn't really "fall down slain" rather they fell down 'alive' and were spared and taken as prisoners.
27	*As for both kings,*	5	Epiphanes and Ptolemy	Okay

95

	their hearts will be intent on mischief, and they will speak lies to each other at the same table	1	They shall, under the semblance of intimacy, at Memphis try to deceive one another	No historical record here by JFB--merely a generalization.
	but it will not succeed,	1	Neither of them shall carry his point at this time.	No historical record here by JFB--merely a generalization.
	for the end is still to come at the appointed time.	5	"the end" of the contest between them is reserved for "the time appointed"	I agree that God appoints the times.
28	*Then he will return to his land with much possessions*	5	On his way back to Syria, he attacked Jerusalem…	Okay
	but his heart will be set against the holy covenant,	5	Epiphanes' army slew 40,000 and took another 40,000 as slaves	Okay
	and he will take action and then return to his own land.	5	He shall effect his purpose. Guided by Menelaus, the high priest, he entered the sanctuary with blasphemies, took away the gold and silver vessels, sacrificed swine on the altar	Okay
29	*At the appointed time*	0	"the time" spoken of in Dan 11:27.	Once again, JFB runs out of battles and interprets this as a repeat of verse 27. No points.
	he will return and come into the South,	0	[continuation]	[same as above]
	but this time it will not happen as the first and as the last.	0	[Here, per JFB: "first" refers back to verse 22 and the 2nd attack in 168 B.C. while "the last" refers forward to verse 42, having nothing to do with Epiphanes.	No points here.
30	*For ships of Kittim will come against him*	0	[JFB applies this also back to verse 22 (see my comments at right) but he can't. He has gone way past verse 22 to try and place this sequentially 8 verses back.]	He is confronted in Alexandria by Roman consul Laenas who demands that he leave or risk attack by Rome. No points here for JFB--interpretation is too scattered about.
	therefore he will be disheartened,	0	[continuation]	True--he left Egypt immediately. Also no points here for the same reason as above.

	and will return and become enraged at the holy covenant and take action	5	Indignant that meantime God's worship had been restored at Jerusalem, he gives vent to his wrath at the check given him by Rome, on the Jews.	His persecutions against the Jewish people begins as recorded in Maccabees
	so he will come back and show regard for those who forsake the holy covenant.	5	namely, with the apostates in the nation (1 Maccabees 1:11-15). Menelaus and other Jews instigated the king against their religion and country	He favors those on his side
31	And forces from him will arise, desecrate the sanctuary fortress,	5	[all of this verse is applied to desecration of the temple]	Historically accurate
	and do away with the regular sacrifice.	5	[ditto]	Historically accurate
	And they will set up the abomination of desolation.	5	[ditto]	Historically accurate
			Here Antiochus' actings are described in language which reach beyond him the type to Antichrist the antitype [JEROME]	**I will stop here and grade JFB on a curve (except for verse 40). JFB apply the remaining verses to Antiochus--IF it seems relevant. Or, they apply it to the Antichrist IF it seems relevant to him. Thus they bounce back and forth between 170 B.C. and 2000+ A.D.**
40	At the end time the king of the South will collide with him, and the king of the North will storm against him with chariots, with horsemen and with many ships and he will enter countries, overflow them and pass through.	0	This Dan 11:40 , therefore, may be a recapitulation summing up the facts of the first expedition to Egypt (171-170 B.C.), in Dan 11:22, 25 and Dan 11:41 , the former invasion of Judea, in Dan 11:28 Dan 11:42, 43 , the second and third invasions of Egypt (169 and 168 B.C.) in Dan 11:23, 24, 29, 30 .	No points for implying that Gabriel forgot to tell Daniel something else.
			Total possible score 96 items x 5 pts. Each =480	**JFB's Score = 261 = 54% JFB's Grade = F**

Daniel Chapter 11—Comments on the Commentary* of
JOHN F. WALVOORD

* Daniel- The Key to Prophetic Revelation, 1971, Moody Bible Institute.

Verse Number	Scriptural Portion—NASB	Walvoord Score	My Comment
2	And now I will tell you the truth. Behold, three more kings are going to arise in Persia.	5	I agree
	Then a fourth will gain for more riches than all of them;	5	I agree
	as soon as he becomes strong through his riches, he will arouse the whole empire against the realm of Greece.	5	I agree
3	And a mighty king will arise, and he will rule with great authority and do as he pleases	5	I agree
4	But as soon as he has arisen,	5	I agree
	his kingdom will be broken up and parceled out toward the four winds of the heaven	5	I agree--the four generals of Alexander the Great
	though not to his own descendants,	5	I agree--not to his only heir, Alexander.
	nor according to his authority which he wielded;	5	I agree--"did not preserve the glory and power it had in Alexander's day." And see next verse.
	for his sovereignty will be uprooted and given to others besides these.	0	No comment here by Walvoord. After stating that the empire would be carved-up into four pieces, Daniel states that *"it will be given to others besides these."* And by obvious reference--given to others besides the four generals.
5	Then the king of the South	1	Walvoord makes several inconsistent statements without explanation:
			1) He states, *"In verse 8, the king of the south is identified as Egypt"*--with no explanation as to why Daniel uses an enigmatic name here.

			2) He states, *"Syria is not mentioned by name [since it no longer existed] and such a reference would be confusing."* But Syria *had* existed before the time of Daniel. Why would the reference to this same land be confusing? Isn't the phrase "king of the north" confusing?
			3) In inconsistent logic, Walvoord fails to mention that at the time of Daniel's writing, Greece did not, nor had not existed! The city states of Athens, Sparta, and Marathon existed and fought with each other but the empire of Greece would not come on the scene for another 500 years--yet no one finds that confusing.
	will grow strong	5	He identifies Ptolemy I Soter as the king of the south here--okay.
	along with one of his princes	0	He identifies Seleucus I Nicator, a king of equal standing, as "one of his princes." Also, he fails to identify who the other "princes" were who had apparent equal standing with Seleucus.
	who will gain ascendancy over him and obtain a great dominion	2	Partial credit: Seleucus I Nicator did become stronger, but not "over" Ptolemy. They were still allies though their offspring were not.
	his domain will be a great (vast) dominion indeed.	1	By superlative reference with verse 4, his dominion will be *"vast indeed"* that is--even surpassing Alexander's. Walvoord makes a reverse comment regarding this.
6	*And after some years (lit. "...in the end of years...")*	5	Walvoord identifies ~50 years as *"some years"*--will he remain consistent?
	they will form an alliance, and the daughter of the king of the South will come to the king of the North to carry out a peaceful arrangement.	3	True, there was an alliance formed by the marriage. But the passage indicates that the arrangement was instigated by the daughter--not by her father Ptolemy II as stated by Walvoord.
	But she will not retain her position of power, nor will he remain with his power	2	Partial credit: Berenice had no power. She was the unwilling pawn in the marriage to Antiochus II. No explanation for, "…nor will he remain with his power."
	but she will be given up, along with those who brought her in	5	Walvoord defines *"given up"* as "murdered"--in this case by a vengeful ex-wife.
	and the one who sired her (HNV-"became a father to her"),	2	In this case, *"given up"* is redefined by Walvoord as Ptolemy II "dying of natural causes and old age." Inconsistent interpretation--though he did die.

	as well as he who supported her in those times.	4	Her husband Antiochus II--in what way did he "support" her?
7	But one of her branch of her roots	3	Technically a brother IS a branch out of the same roots as Berenice, but the passage seems to imply a familial connection that is far more distant. Why not just say "her brother" if that was what was intended?
	will arise in his place	5	Prince Ptolemy III becomes "king" of Egypt.
	and he will come against their army and enter the fortress (or "place of strength") of the king of the North and he will deal with them and display great strength.	5	Ptolemy III invades Syria, occupies Antioch, and even reaches Babylon. This was the height of Ptolemaic power--and its greatest extent. This was the "Third Syrian War." One wonders why Daniel does not mention the first two campaigns if this Greek history was so important.
8	And also their gods with their metal images and their precious vessels of silver and gold he will take into captivity to Egypt,	5	Walvoord's explanation is sufficient but does lack historical detail. However, his quotation from Jerome supplies the detail here.
	and he on his part will refrain from attacking the king of the North for some years.	3	Ptolemy III did indeed cease from any further attacks against Syria. However, the phrase "for some years" literally means *"a division of time."* Ptolemy would start the 4th Syrian war 22 years later--not a very precise *"division of time."* Also, he is inconsistent with his previous definition of "some years" being equal to 50 years in verse six.
9	Then the latter will enter the realm of the king of the South, but will return to his own land.	4	Seleucus II Callinicus did retake some of northern Syria and Iran but lost the areas in a battle with his brother. A rather insignificant event considering the lack of reference to other, much more major battles.
10	And his sons will mobilize and assemble a multitude of great forces...	3	Walvoord identifies only one son (Seleucus III) before Antiochus III the Great succeeds in defeating Ptolemy as he identifies in the next portion of the verse. Where are the *"multitude" (plural) "of forces" (also plural)?*
	...and one of them will keep coming and overflow and pass through, that he may again wage war up to his very fortress.	4	"…one of them…" one of whom? Per JFB, one of the sons of the king of the north shall "keep coming." However, this Battle of Raphia was started, not by the Seleucid's of the north, but by Ptolemy Philopater of the south.
11	And the king of the South will be enraged and go forth and fight with the king of the North.	5	Ptolemy Philopater returns the attack against Antiochus III and defeats him at the Battle of Raphia.

100

	Then the latter will raise a great multitude,	4	*Most* translations indicate this to be a subsequent event caused by the previous battle. However, the KJV used by Walvoord does not, and I will concede the point on a technicality.
	but that multitude will be given into the hand of the former.	5	The forces of Antiochus III were defeated by the Egyptians at Raphia. Antiochus escapes.
12	*When the multitude is carried away, his heart will be lifted up, and he will cause tens of thousands to fall;*	2	Walvoord makes no direct reference to this portion but seems to believe that Daniel is repeating what he already wrote in verse 11.
	yet he will not prevail.	0	He believes that it is the self indulgence of Philopater that caused him not to pursue his advantage here--thus he was not *"strengthened by it."* However, 8 other translations (including the NKJV) translate this as *"he will not prevail."* Indicating that even though his army was triumphant, he himself was defeated. Also, in contrasting his interpretation of this verse to actual history, Philopater DID *prevail* at the battle of Raphia. So much so that Antiochus withdrew from Judea all the way north to Lebanon.
13	*For the king of the North will again raise a greater multitude than the former,*	5	Ptolemy IV dies and Ptolemy V Epiphanes gains the throne at the age of five. Antiochus III rebuilds his army. He invades Coele-Syria and begins the 5th Syrian War.
	and at the end of the times	0	Walvoord makes no comment here, *"certain years"* (KJV) here would have been 18 years since the Battle of Raphia. However, the literal meaning is "at the end time of the times [even of] years." It means at the end of an epoch or event; or at the end of a fixed unit of time such as decade, century, etc.
	he will press on with a great army and much equipment.	4	Antiochus III retakes Syria and Phoenicia.
14	*Now in those times many will rise up against the king of the South;*	4	Walvoord makes no mention of it, but during this time the Egyptian Revolt took place. Upper Egypt seceded from the Ptolemaic Empire. It is a valid point that I would make if I were arguing FOR this interpretation.
	the violent ones among your people will also lift themselves up in order to fulfill the vision,	2	Here, he interprets this as: '...*the violent ones will lift themselves up which will inadvertently have the future effect of fulfilling the vision of the Jewish affliction yet to come under Antiochus Epiphanes.*' I believe that this is quite a stretch from the intended meaning of: '*the violent ones will lift themselves up in order that they might cause <u>their own vision</u> for the Jewish people to become fulfilled.*'

	but they will fall down.	0	No explanation here by Walvoord. But continuing *his* interpretation: if they were not successful in fulfilling the vision (i.e. they *"fall down"* in their attempt) does this mean that the Jewish affliction would not take place? Which it obviously did.
15	*Then the king of the North will come, cast up a siege mound,*	0	The next historical battle between Antiochus III and Ptolemy's general Scopus occurred at the Battle of Paneas, near the headwaters of the Jordan. The battle was out on the open plain---there was no siege mound
	and capture a well fortified city;	0	Though Scopus fled to Sidon where he was finally captured; the battle was well over by then and Antiochus already had control of Phoenicia and the port of Sidon.
	and the forces of the South will not stand their ground, not even their choicest troops, for there will be no strength to make a stand.	2	His interpretation here is the unsuccessful attempt by three Egyptian leaders to rescue Scopus from Sidon. However, this was a rescue attempt-- *'standing their ground'* was not even possible since they had lost their ground.
16	*But he who comes against him will do as he pleases,*	0	No comment here by Walvoord. Someone, but obviously not the king of the south, comes against the king of the north and does as he pleases. Who is this third party?
	and no one will be able to withstand him;	0	Again, no explanation here by Walvoord as to who this third, most powerful force might be.
	he will stay for a time in the beautiful land,	0	Again, no explanation here by Walvoord.
	by which his hand shall be consumed.	0	Again, no explanation here by Walvoord.
17	*And he will set his face to come with the power of his whole kingdom,*	0	No definitive explanation here by Walvoord, but assume that he believes this refers here to the next phrase.
	bringing with him an equitable arrangement which he will put into effect;	5	Antiochus III is forced by Rome to make peace with the Ptolemies.
	he will also give him the daughter of women	5	He gives his daughter Cleopatra I Syra (not the famous one--she was the 7th) to Ptolemy V Epiphanes
	but she will be ruined by it.	3	Interprets this as: she will (hopefully) ruin Ptolemy's kingdom.
	But she will not take a stand for him or be on his side.	5	She always sided with her young, 16-year-old, husband, Ptolemy V.
18	*Then he will turn his face to the coastlands and capture many.*	0	Antiochus *does* attempt to recapture Greece but is NOT successful. He does not *"capture many."*

	But a commander will put a stop to his scorn against him;	5	He is stopped by the Roman general Scipio. Antiochus had shown contempt for Rome's ambassadors.
	moreover, he will repay him for his scorn.	5	He is defeated by Scipio. After the battle of Magnesia, he signs the Treaty of Apamea, promising never to return to Europe among other conditions.
19	*So he will turn his face toward the fortresses of his own land,*	1	Per Walvoord, a repeat of turning *"his face to the coastlands"* in verse 18. Antiochus turns his face back to Greece to conquer. That the description of the event should be repeated within two succeeding verses defies explanation.
	but he will stumble and fall and be found no more.	5	As stated, he is unsuccessful in attempting to capture Greece.
20	*Then in his place one will arise who will send a tax collector through the jewel of his kingdom;*	5	Seleucus IV Philopater replaces Antiochus III. He is forced to raise taxes for Rome.
	yet within a few days he will be broken, though neither in anger nor in battle.	2	All interpretations agree that Philopater was murdered, but it is difficult to interpret murder as not being done in anger.
21	*And in his place a despicable person will arise,*	5	The rise of Antiochus IV Epiphanes--the despicable ruler because of verse 31. However, one fact of history seems to belie his title regarding the Jews, Epiphanes paid for the Septuagint Translation of the Hebrew Scriptures into Greek.
	on whom the honor of kingship has not been conferred,	2	Walvoord and others claim that Epiphanes "seized the throne rather than obtaining it honorably," as if this was something new.
	but he will come in a time of tranquility and seize the kingdom by intrigue.	5	Epiphanes did seize the kingdom by intrigue, deception, and murder--just like his ancestors.
22	*And the overflowing forces*	1	Walvoord fails to identify any "overflowing" forces. The most powerful army at the time was Rome, and Epiphanes was not foolhardy enough to challenge them.
	will be flooded away before him and shattered,	2	Epiphanes has some skirmishes with the Ptolemies, now a vassal state of Rome. He is forced to treat them with kid-gloves to keep from inciting wrath from Rome. "Shattered"---hardly.
	and also the prince of the covenant.	5	Here he identifies the Jewish, high priest Onias as the "prince of the covenant".

23	*And after an alliance is made with him he will practice deception*	0	Walvoord (and history) fail to define or record any alliances that he made with other nations. He does invade Egypt twice, but Walvoord spends these invasions as fulfillment of succeeding verses.
	and he will go up and gain power with a small force of people.	0	Epiphanes is boxed-in to his present geographic state by Rome in the west and Parthia in the east. He does not gain any more power than what has already been stated.
24	*In a time of tranquility*	5	The *Pax Romana* prevailed during this time.
	he will enter [fall upon] the richest parts of the realm,	0	Walvoord correctly interprets this as a battle--yet he has run out of battles. He tries to tie this to verse 25, yet these are a succession of chronological events as indicated by the repeat of the conjunctional phrase "and he will..."
	and he will accomplish what his fathers never did, nor his ancestors;	2	Walvoord claims that Epiphanes' ancestors never used the spoils of war to bribe others to join the cause. However, in the next portion, quoting from Maccabees he contradicts this assertion. His ancestors did give gifts--just not as lavishly as Epiphanes.
	he will distribute plunder, booty, and possessions among them,	5	Quoting from Maccabees 3:30, Epiphanes is recorded to have given lavish gifts, more so than his ancestors.
	and he will devise his schemes against strongholds, but only for a time.	0	No comment here by Walvoord.
25	*And he will stir up his strength and courage against the king of the South with a large army;*	4	Hardly a major battle. The Ptolemy brothers were in the midst of a struggle for supremacy among each other. Ptolemy's guardians were demanding that Epiphanes return Syria to Ptolemaic rule sparking a preemptive strike by Epiphanes. He overruns the entire country and captures Ptolemy VI.
	so the king of the South will mobilize an extremely large and mighty army for war;	1	Not really. From the historical narratives, though there was no doubt some fighting, the South did not *"mobilize an extremely large and mighty army for war."*

	but he will not stand, for schemes will be devised against him.	2	Ptolemy did not stand--he was captured. There is no record of schemes being devised against him.
26	*And those who eat his choice food will break him,*	1	No historical record here by Walvoord--merely a generalization.
	and his army will be swept away	5	Ptolemy's army offered little resistance.
	and many will fall down slain.	1	Not really.
27	*As for both kings,*	5	Epiphanes and Ptolemy
	their hearts will be intent on mischief, and they will speak lies to each other at the same table;	1	No historical record here by Walvoord--merely a generalization.
	but it will not succeed,	1	No historical record here by Walvoord--merely a generalization.
	time.	5	I agree that God appoints the times.
28	*Then he will return to his land with much possessions;*	1	No historical record here by Walvoord--merely a generalization.
	but his heart will be set against the holy covenant,	5	Epiphanes hated the Jews--the stage is being set for "the abomination of desolation."
	and he will take action and then return to his own land.	0	No historical record here by Walvoord--merely a generalization.
29	*At the appointed time*	5	I agree that God appoints the times.
	he will return and come into the South,	0	Walvoord defines this as the 2nd invasion of Egypt which he already spent on verse 25.
	but this time it will not happen as the first and as the last.	5	This time Epiphanes is not successful as defined in the next verses…
30	*For ships of Kittim will come against him;*	5	He is confronted in Alexandria by Roman consul Laenas who demands that he leave or risk attack by Rome.
	therefore he will be disheartened,	5	True--he left Egypt immediately
	and will return and become enraged at the holy covenant and take action;	5	His persecutions against the Jewish people begin as recorded in Maccabees
	so he will come back and show regard for those who forsake the holy covenant.	5	He favors those on his side

105

31	*And forces from him will arise, desecrate the sanctuary fortress,*	5	Historically accurate
	and do away with the regular sacrifice.	5	Historically accurate
	And they will set up the abomination of desolation.	5	Historically accurate
32	*And by smooth words he will turn to godlessness those who act wickedly toward the covenant,*	2	No comment of historical record here by Walvoord--but most likely true.
	but the people who know their God will display strength and take action.	2	No comment of historical record here by Walvoord--but most likely true.
33	*And those who have insight among the people will give understanding to the many;*	2	No comment of historical record here by Walvoord--but most likely true.
	yet they will fall by sword and by flame, by captivity and by plunder, for many days.	2	No comment of historical record here by Walvoord--but most likely true.
34	*Now when they fall they will be granted a little help,*	2	No comment of historical record here by Walvoord--but most likely true.
	and many will join them in hypocrisy.	5	King Herod was of the Maccabees family.
35	*And some of those who have insight will fall,*	2	No comment of historical record here by Walvoord--but most likely true.
	in order to refine, purge, and make them white, until the end time;	2	No comment of historical record here by Walvoord--but most likely true.
	because it is still to come at the appointed time.	2	No comment of historical record here by Walvoord--but most likely true.

Here, according to Walvoord (and others) the prophetic *River of Time* vanishes into a canyon--unable to be seen by Old Testament prophets until the "time of the end" prior to Christ's 2nd advent. The verses that follow are applied to the Antichrist and the end times.

Total possible score 104 items x 5 pts. Each = 520		**Walvoord's Score = 311 = 59% Walvoord's Grade = F**